PRAISE FOR RUTH KRALL

Ruth Krall is known as a tireless scholar, a beloved professor, and a fearless advocate for sexual abuse survivors. In *Inanna's Way*, we learn to know a private side of Ruth: her battle with a serious and painful illness. Using the Sumerian myth of the Goddess Inanna's descent to the Underworld as a metaphor, through word and image, Ruth gives us a peek at the many "gates" through which she passed, facing and then shedding her despair and anger at feeling betrayed by her own body, and finally her long journey to healing.

— CAMERON ALTARAS

Cameron Altaras, PhD, Editor, with Carol Penner,
Resistance: Confronting Violence, Power and Abuse Within Peace Churches;
Author, with Sharla Nafziger,
Confronting the Patterns that Silence Us

Few people would even attempt to transform the lessons of physical tragedy into such profound creating and writing. But Ruth Krall's capacity for deep reflection and renewal is nothing short of heroic. With care and humility, Ruth offers her story of pain and empowerment through these poems — a gift for all to turn to and treasure.

— ANNA GROFF

Anna M. Groff is the Associate Professor of Communication,
Goshen College, Goshen, IN

In *Inanna's Way*, Ruth Krall takes us on the heroine's journey, following the mythic Sumerian goddess through the underworld to resurrection. Tracing her progress from surgery to recovery, she offers a series of poems and masks that illustrate her observation that "transformation is always possible." These words and images project the "numinous power of an ancient narrative" to renew and sustain life in an everyday world that holds both threat and promise. Inanna's passage through the seven gates of the underworld--represented by seven stunning masks--culminates in death and resurrection, the birth of a new self. Ruth claims Inanna's transformation for herself in an unforgettable memoir.

— JUDITH DAVIS

Judith M. Davis, Ph.D., is professor emerita of French and Humanities at Goshen College (Indiana). A frequent presenter at scholarly conferences, she is the author of *Finding the Virgin Mary: Her Evolving Stories from Antiquity to Today* as well as two other volumes in medieval studies.

INANNA'S WAY

A Personal Journey into the Underworld

RUTH KRALL

ISBN: 978-1-990827-22-8

Cover design by Gelassenheit Publications, Ltd., with use of the author's photographs of the mask collection, found throughout the poems in this volume. The front cover is set in a modified photograph of the huluppu tree. (https://www.mesopotamiangods.com/the-huluppu-tree/)

Includes Bibliographic References

1. Poetry
2. Mask Photography
3. Inanna, Goddess of Ancient Sumer
4. Healing after a life-threatening Illness
5. Trauma Recovery

2nd Edition

First Printing in the United States of America
First Electronic Publication on the World Wide Web
Enduring Space Publications
Tucson, AZ 85747

Second printed edition by Gelassenheit Publications, Ltd.
St Catharines, Ohnia:kara, Ontario, Canada

IN MEMORY

Jeevan Paul, M. D.

Bob Bernard
Nancy Burke
Kirby Gross
John Harley
Marcy Clark Lee
Judy Martin
Emmett E. Miller
Larry Smith
Jon Smucker

CONTENTS

THE POETRY

IN APPRECIATION

I am filled with love and gratitude for the healers who worked with me in a healing team. Judy Martin, Emmett Miller, Nancy Burke and Marcy Clark Lee not only touched my wounded body with competency, they helped restore my spirit. In addition, however, not every healer has body-healing credentials. But they are healers nonetheless. For voice coach and teacher Bob Bernard's gifts to me, I am especially grateful. As my body healed, he gave me music. In his voice studio I sang and laughed and began once more to believe in my body's wisdom and abilities. Atlee Beechy, Howard Clinebell, Molly Engle, Ed Gelardin and Jeevan Paul all served as guardians of my spirit as I began hypnotic work. Understanding my fear of the process, they read and wrote frequent letters and emails. We talked by phone and in person. They heard the story as it unraveled itself. They watched over me while I unraveled myself.

I am grateful to colleagues and friends who read early drafts of this work or watched the mask-making unfold. They offered encouragement, and made helpful suggestions. At various times each of the following freely offered me help and advice: Atlee Beechy, Beth Martin Birky, Todd Davis, Charlotte Ellen, Molly Engle, Martha Smith Good, Ellen Hackman, Gayle Gerber Koontz, Dawn Bontrager, Peggy Lesniewicz, Mary Linton, Jeevan Paul, Meribeth Shank, Priscilla Stuckey, Laura Weaver, and Judy

Wenig Horswell. Angeles Arrien, Emmett Miller, and Dwight Judy read early drafts of the manuscript and their kind comments gave me courage to continue shaping the material. Judith Davis read a very late draft of the entire manuscript and made invaluable contributions to the clarity of the prose text. Rafael and Christine Falcón helped me with the Spanish subtitles but any errors in my use of my second language are mine. Rachel Lapp and Matthew Murschel carefully photographed the majority of the masks. Floyd Saner helped with digital photography and assisted me with integration of the mask photographs into the text. I am grateful, as well, to Peggy Fox and Patty Callahan. Their neighborly friendship and support as I created mask after mask in our shared outdoor space helped to sustain me during a year of great emotional chaos and confusion. Marge Pacer's and Michelle Lucchese's enthusiasm cheered me on when I wondered if Inanna should "attempt to make her way into the world."

The assistance of reference librarians at Goshen College in Goshen, Indiana and at the Graduate Theological Union in Berkeley, California was essential and I am grateful for their professional expertise and friendly helpfulness in locating resources.

One of these poems, *Birthing Woman*, has been previously published in Miller, Alicia M., *Ephemeris: Journeys to Becoming a Modern Mennonite Woman as captured in essays and journal entries* (Goshen, IN: an FTP book, 2002). Appreciation is expressed for permission to re-place this poem in the sequence from which it was taken for the Miller collection. Several of the poems were combined, redacted, edited and published in Stotlzfus, M., Green, R., and Schumm, D. (eds.), *Chronic Illness, Spirituality and Healing: Diverse Disciplinary, Religious and Cultural Perspectives* (New York, NY: Palgreave-Macmillan, 2013). Appreciation is expressed for permission to re-place these poetry segments in the sequence from which they were abstracted.

I want to express specific appreciation to the Eli Lilly Foundation, Inc., of Indianapolis, Indiana for providing me with a Lilly Open Faculty Fellowship during my 1995 -1996 sabbatical as a scholar-in-residence at the Graduate Theological Union in Berkeley. The irony of my sabbatical's topic of study, chosen nearly a year before the biopsy revealed my body's malignancy, was never lost to me. For that proposed study, *Liturgy as Destroyer – Liturgy as Healer*, the Lilly Foundation had funded me to examine the healing potential of religious and medical liturgies. The intersection of my professional interests in healing and my personal need to find healing was most serendipitous. Both illumined both; each illumining the other.

After my second surgery resulted in a very large seroma,[1] I asked the presiding surgeon, Jon Smucker, "Must I now cancel my sabbatical year?" He wisely said, "Of course not. It is your body that is wounded, not your mind. You can study there as well as here. Your body can heal there as well as here." My faculty colleague, Ann Hostetler was helpful to me in pointing out that healing the body's open wound from the inside out could also be a metaphor for body-mind therapeutic work done with tools of hypnotic regression.

In August 1995, my niece, Beth Krall, drove with me to Berkeley and we set off on the adventure that would lead to my rediscovery of Inanna's Sumerian story. Beth's decision to travel west with me made my decision to do the sabbatical as scheduled much easier for me. In August 1996, Jeevan Paul flew to Berkeley at the end of the sabbatical year and drove me home. Because of his kindness, I had time in the car to think about how to integrate the sabbatical year's events and intellectual work into my continuing life.

April, 2004

1. A seroma is a technical medical word to describe a sterile accumulation of body fluids. In my situation a large collection of fluids near the abdominal incision burst open approximately two weeks after surgery. The body now needed to heal itself by its own healing means – from the inside out.

AUTHOR'S PREFATORY NOTE

VICTORY WITH TWO TRUMPETS

Inanna's Way bears testimony to the life force that flows in and through each one of us and that will continue to flow when any one of us has returned our bodies to the dust from which we were created. It is life herself that has borne us out of the womb of past generations. It is life herself that continues to give birth to itself in succeeding generations. For this moment we are simply a manifested vessel of consciousness into which life has poured flesh, breath and spirit. For this time we know as our life, we are simply a water skin of life's consciousness. Life moves in and through us as life wills. Life brings us breath, and for as long as we live, life continues to breathe in us.

We participate in life by living but we cannot control the life force as she moves among us, breathing into each one of us and bringing us to consciousness. When our own individual life ceases to be breathed, life will continue to bring consciousness into all subsequent manifestations of its ongoing being and becoming.

When reading this book's contemporary retelling of an ancient Sumerian narrative, listen to it with an open heart. Accept this story of the Sumerian goddess Inanna into your heart and know her story mirrors many shapes of suffering and transformation, many seasons of shattering and metamorphosis. In hearing Inanna's story whispered through my words, listen for your own story. In honoring Inanna's journey, honor your own.

Every individual life knows times of death, suffering, and loss as well as times of resurrection and reanimation of the life force. No human individual can escape the underworld's wisdom for life.

As you read my retelling of this ancient story of Inanna's journey into the underworld of death, have compassion for yourself. Open your own spirit and heart to know and understand your personal and unique journeys through life's continuous cycles of loss, grief, and transformation. Inanna's passage from life into the bleak underworld of death teaches us about giving ourselves over to life's important work with us.

Inanna's passage from the underworld back into life provides us with an important foreknowing. Even when we are most trapped in awareness of our own suffering, we need to know that our continuing life contains the present moment of transcendence. Transformation is always possible.

Because we love life; because we love others; because we love ourselves: each of us must cut open our own trails through the wilderness of suffering. The moment when the wildness of our suffering closes in around us is the moment when we know we are lost. In the moment that we realize we have lost our way, we concomitantly find ourselves standing in strange doorways that both beckon to us and repel us. Having entered the pathway into the dark night of the soul, we discover altars in places where we least anticipate shrines and burial vaults where we most desire to worship life.

Upon entering into life-changing boundary situations, we begin, if we are wise, to prepare for an arduous journey. In the moment when we hear the voices of our own underworld calling us, we know that they call us by our many names. Intuitively we realize that we are trapped into a journey we would avoid if at all possible. However, upon hearing these underworld voices calling us, we know immediately that there is no way to avoid them.

There is no way to avoid making the journey into the dark night of our suffering.

Sensing that hard times lie ahead for us, we mobilize our resources so that others may watch over us. No one, it is true, can walk through the overgrown wilderness thickets for us. No one can even walk with us through our personal gates of suffering. But, knowing that we are lovingly attended to and watched over, we find hope that we may be able to find an honorable way to travel into the depths of suffering, and in those depths, find healing.

Tossed against the doorway of suffering, we intuit that our journey will change us, and our perception of the world, forever. Times of life-threatening illness; times when we lose our powers in the world; times of strong grief; times of great fear; times of struggle with the unnamed and unknowable: these are all times of hearing the call of the world of death. Each of these experiences can provide the impetus for us to explore our own underworld of the shadows and the shades. Each of these can take us into nether worlds whose meaning to us is so deep we have no words adequate for the task of making our way.

As we struggle with the inner chaos of voicelessness, wordlessness and fear, we realize the nearly total loss of our powers of control in the world. As we struggle with the absence of adequate maps, oracles, portents and prophecies, we discover that it is imperative to make friends with our ongoing existential experiences of pain, anxiety, terror, rage, and despair. We discover, as we journey that we must face and acknowledge the inner experience which so devastates us and lays waste to our usual powers in the world. In our sense of lostness, we realize we must make peace with the experience of being lost. We must do all of this inner work, we realize, because our struggles, our difficult life experiences, and the sense of being totally lost are the only reliable guides to our inner journey.

Somewhere in the wilderness (or the bleak arid desert) of our own particular journey into the soul's dark night, we begin to reflect on our life and our current troubles. In these actual moments of memory, turmoil, panic, and despair, we attempt to hold onto sustaining memories of centeredness, groundedness, security and joy. We search through our memories and ask them to teach us what they can. We longingly recall moments when we knew a secure inner calmness of being.

We begin, then, to create meaning out of this present moment of suffering. In our intense self-examination, something deep stirs within us and we remember what it was like to feel well and whole. We stretch towards that remembered wholeness with intense desire. No longer totally separated from our own self; no longer totally alienated from the life force that continues to live in us; no longer sensing our absolute separation from others: we slowly open ourselves to whatever it will be that finds us and heals us. In that moment of surrender and opening, a well of healing waters shows itself to us and we begin to drink.

Tasting the remembered artesian waters of life, we recognize that our journey has already changed us and is continuing to change us. We recognize that we are a metamorphosis in process. With this recognition, we begin the slow acknowledgment to ourselves and others that we can never return to who we were in the moment just before our journey into life's underworld began.

A wild grief erupts because we are no longer who we were. A rough-handed terror claims us because we do not yet know who we are now. Dread invades and shadows our brooding because we cannot know the outcome of our journey until it is completed. We feel the psychic tug of our wounds and scars. Simultaneously, however, we feel the strong tug of the life force calling us forward.

There is no way to successfully abort the journey and return to wholeness. The only way to find a full, abundant and living life is to continue. The only way to return to the upper world of the living is to yield to the transforming processes of the underworld – those processes of dying and resurrection that continuously move in and through us.

The path out of the wilderness of suffering begins with this time of inner reflection. The way begins with our own deep inner processes of searching for the meaning of suffering in our particular life. In this time of reflection and deep searching we eventually learn to trust our personal experience. We eventually learn to honor suffering's wisdom for our lives. Gradually we come to accept the presence of suffering as our most reliable guide through the wildness of the dark night into which life has tossed us.

In learning to be present to the experience of suffering as our teacher and guide, we begin to intuit a deeper experience of joy that travels with us as well. We are not only suffering and dying. We are being reborn into life. We begin to recognize that each moment in which life breathes us into being, we are embodied life. Life not only suffers in us and with us. Life also rejoices in us and in itself. Even in the midst of the chaos of not knowing whether we shall live or die; in the midst of not knowing whether we shall succeed or fail miserably in our search for life: life herself pours the waters of healing all around us. In the moments of our journey when healing flows into us and through us; in the moments when the waters of life connect with us: we enter into moments of truthful resurrection.

Immersed in the healing waters of life, we find a song singing us. It is the song of life and as long as we breathe it is always present within us. Hearing the song of life singing deeply within our consciousness, we begin to sing our own song back. We sing and life sings back. Life sings and we sing back. In our unique song of life, we encounter embodied joy.

If we are to emerge from these deep, gray, wordless underworlds — our encounters with life's difficult will for us — we must bow before the gates of death and pray that the vital song of the lifeforce has not forgotten us. The sorrows and losses that we take into the land beyond words must become our teachers if we are to live equitably with their terrifying presence. In the moment of acceptance of our situation exactly as it is (no more and no less), our sorrows and our losses become our transforming powers.

To hear our own song, indeed to hear life's song, within us in the midst of suffering, we must become quiet and still within our spirit. When we reach a certain stillness, suffering begins to yield to acceptance. Acceptance allows us to ask of suffering what it will teach us. In that moment, the healing waters of life flow unrestricted through us and around us. We find that we are not alone. Life, Herself, is with us. Recognizing Her we are overcome by joy.

This is the wisdom of Inanna's journey into the underworld to meet her older sister Ereshkigal. This is the wisdom of our own stories of moving into our own underworld stories. The cycle of life is a continuously moving circle of living and dying; of dying and living. Accepting this, we begin a journey of deep, inner transformation. In this journey, suffering gives way to acceptance and joy. As long as we live, life is with us. Understanding this, we come to understand that life moves always within us to bring us renewed life. As we accept the realities of our life exactly as they are we begin to understand that all life is sacred. Life's sorrows, suffering, grief, pain, rage, terror, and despair are sacred in their ordinary presence within our lives. As we reach deep within ourselves to find the resources to survive suffering, we discover that it is not only in the good and happy times of our lives that we discover life's amazing steadfastness to us.

As we make cyclical journeys into life's more dense realities of suffering, we find life is there with us as well. A deep abiding joy sustains us and allows us to find and use our remaining powers.

Personal Responses

In my own personal encounter with life's difficult will for my own life journey, I re-met the Sumerian goddess Inanna. I studied Bronze Age texts for their wisdom for my own life. I found a remarkable myth whose wisdom guided me in a terrifying 18 months of my life.

In 1995 I survived two surgeries that followed a biopsy report of endometrial cancer. The first surgery removed the malignancy. After getting fully awake from anesthesia, the surgeon told me that no malignant cells were found outside the uterus. He told me he thought I had an excellent chance of living for a long time. I set myself to the business of recovering from the dual assault of surgery and anesthesia. I began walking every day. I rested. I ate healthy foods. I accepted immediately the opinion that I would live. Joy at being alive flowed into me and through me like a strong springtime river. Joy invaded my spirit. Joy sustained me in the first days after surgery. I would live.

The surgical wound, however, did not heal well. It herniated and I needed to return again into surgery. Following the repair of the herniated wound, I again moved back into restorative actions: walking, sleeping, visiting with friends, and eating healthy foods.

Almost a month after the hernia repair, the wound opened once more. This time I had an open wound, an abdominal seroma. The surgeon told me that the body's open wound would need to heal itself. In short, I would live with an open body wound while the body itself directed my healing. I would not be re-sewn. No physician would preside over my healing. Instead, I would need to wait for the body to heal itself.

For more than a year I lived with an open abdominal wound that steadily and slowly healed. But its scarring was deep and permanent. Each day during those months the body's wounds called me insistently to care for my inner spirit's wounds.

In the years before my malignancy was diagnosed, I had lived in grief. In each of the preceding six years, someone of great importance to my life had died or an important relationship had failed. I had tried to do my grief work with each death or loss, but when a college classmate and close friend Janet Shellenberger died at age 50 from breast cancer, I was bereft. I was overwhelmed by staggering, wordless grief. I simply held it inside and carried it as my own share of the world's grief. I had no language skills capable of speaking what was my inner world.

My own diagnosis followed her death by five weeks. I was initially quite sure that I was going to follow her into the land of death. But each time I heard that thought in my head, I simultaneously found a strong desire to live. I did something that was uncharacteristic of my personality. I reached out to all of my friends and colleagues and said, "Ask your own gods that I might live." I explored the realms of conventional and alternative possibilities. I began a series of therapeutic touch sessions. In one of these sessions, I entered a state of altered consciousness and found a vortex of energy entering my body through the body's center of balance.

During the year following surgery for a malignancy, I held to a strong belief in the power of the life force to bring about physical and emotional healing. Faced with a post-surgery wound that was slow to heal, I entered an underworld of fear of my own body. I was terrified to touch the surgical wound. Before the development of a large abdominal seroma, I had felt invincible. My body always healed well and rapidly.

After the skin of my abdominal surface split open, I was faced with the issue of primary intention healing. I became instantly terrified of my own body. I discovered pure rage at the body for what it was doing to me. One late night when I was alone in my house and frustrated by my now ruined body, I was shocked to hear my very loud voice screaming, "I hate you body for doing this to me." I was so shocked that I retreated into total and withdrawn emotional silence. I immediately understood that this was not the attitude of body-spirit healing. I began to change this spiritual and psychological imagery immediately into one of seeking to cooperate with the body rather than assault it with my rage.

In the midst of all of this emotional upheaval, my body steadily and slowly moved towards healing. The scarring was deep and permanent. Each day during that year, the body's wounds called me to recognize deeper and earlier wounds of the spirit and psyche. With a therapist's help, I confronted out-of-body experiences, a near-death experience, and instances of dissociated terror in childhood.

With the help of my primary healthcare practitioner, I created a complex team of healers. Each of them reassured me that my strong belief in the power of the life force to heal was essential. Each of them acknowledged my terror while not coddling it. Each of them helped me to encode into recognizable language that which previously had been wordless and totally chaotic. In slow steps I entered another form of psychic space, a layer of consciousness I'd not previously encountered or explored. With therapeutic help, I touched more ancient wounds that had left disturbed energy fields in their wake.

Spontaneous healing imagery began to erupt. For several months I imaged the cellular structure of my body being recreated. Every time I cared for my body's wound, I sang an adaptation of a little children's song: *Inch by inch, row by row, gonna help my body grow.* As I sang I imagined healthy cells at work clearing out debris and replacing scar tissue with living cells. I imagined a cellular bricklayer choosing cells and placing them in just the right spaces, leaving no pockets of air or fluid for bacteria to enter and infect the wound.

One day as I sang, I became aware that a large fish was swimming in the open wound of my abdomen. Asking it what it was, it said its name was sturgeon. In the inner, non-rational world of spontaneous imagery, a large sturgeon appeared to help me keep my body wound clean. I knew almost nothing about these great fish. When I talked to my primary care physician, she said something like, "Oh, Ruth, that's wonderful. They are some of the most ancient living organisms that we know. In imagery work, this fish will help you keep your wound clean and healing."

As I continued to work with my body and my psyche, I encountered wells of grief and exploding zones of panic. In doing body-energy work, energy cysts moved and shifted and then drained. I simply tried to stay present to whatever emotional response emerged as I dealt with a body that seemed to have turned on me. When I hit zones of terror and overwhelming sadness, I tried to find the inner lesson. I found the sturgeon's presence in the field of my inner world to be reassuring. As I deliberately and carefully worked with my inner sturgeon, bricklayer and gardener, I also realized that most people would think I'd lost my rational mind.

Sensing a deep inner loss of balance and some unspeakable anguish, each healer encouraged me to seek help in the creative forces that were less dependent upon logical, analytical thought. When poetry began to erupt, each healer was willing to read it and to talk with me about it. When I began to make masks, each healer looked at them with me and sought to uncover their messages.

Sensing a primitive mix of confusing emotions (rage, despair and unremitting anxiety), each healer encouraged me to find the way into my terrors and to believe that I was strong enough to make it through the land of the living dead back into the land of the fully living.

In the middle of my recovery year, in a moment of synchronicity, I traveled to a professional meeting in philosophy and medicine at Pacific Medical Center in San Francisco and heard Jungian analyst Jean Shinoda Bolen read from her 1996 book, *Close to the Bone.* I later did a one day workshop with her on the Dominican College Campus in San Rafael. In these large groups of nurses and physicians, she described the myth of Inanna's journey as one that could be used to help individuals as they made their journey into illness. In the middle of her lectures she described a friend's encounter with cancer. For her woman friend the mythic Inanna and her recorded journey into the underworld was a journey that brought understanding and comfort. As a Jungian analyst Bolen recommended the myth's teachings to the assembled physicians, nurses and other healers.

In *Close to the Bone: Life Threatening Illness and the Search for Meaning,* Bolen elaborates upon her intuitions about the importance of Inanna's journey as a way to conceptualize the chthonic (underworldly) realities of illness which compromises the body-spirit-psyche integrity of the person who is ill.

> Metaphorically and actually, illness and hospitalization strip us of what covered and protected us in many ways…the journey is similar to Inanna's. There are still gates we go through which strip us of persona and defense; we become exposed and bare-souled. The stripping away makes it possible for us to reach depths within ourselves that we might otherwise not reach, where whatever we consigned there or abandoned or forgot of ourselves suffers the pain of not being remembered or of not being integrated into our conscious personality or allowed expression. (*Close to the Bone,* pp. 31-32)

Having heard Bolen's brief lecture references to Inanna, I began to research the goddess and her narrative. As a theologian and former seminary student, I already knew about Inanna and her importance. However, until the evening of Bolen's speech, Inanna was simply one of the bronze-age deities who populated the world of antiquity. Listening to Bolen speak, I immediately and profoundly found Inanna's story to be compelling.

For nearly eighteen months after hearing Bolen's lecture, I went on an intellectual treasure hunt – a hunt in which I sought twentieth-century traces of Inanna. I located literature about myth and legend. I studied narratives about ancient religions and sacred rituals. I researched and read the works of contemporary spiritual healers. I devoured religious and medical literature about dark nights of the soul.

In search of Inanna's actual story in her own culture, I sought out today's translations of Sumer's cuneiform tablets. In addition, I read contemporary adaptations of the myth. I hunted symbolic and artistic renderings of Inanna from within her ancient Sumerian context and from my own context of contemporary Western Christendom. In my studies I found that Inanna has captured the imagination of several additional women healers who see her carrying and representing archetypal wisdom for today's women.

Now, years later, I understand that I was hunting language and symbols to describe what I had experienced in such primitive and narrativeless ways. In a certain sense, looking back, I did that which I have always done when overwhelmed by the demands of my life. I went in search of information about human encounters with the healing gods. I surrounded my life with the wisdom traditions of religion and religious experience. I sought the intuitive and symbolic wisdom of the aesthetic traditions of art and literature. I located skilled healers inside and outside of allopathic (Western) medicine and reflected on their writing and teaching. I wanted to learn, from the position of the one needing healing, what they knew about healing the body and healing the spirit.

What I did not expect in the midst of all of this restless intellectual searching, however, was that I would be so seized by the numinous power of an ancient narrative. I did not, at the beginning of my intellectual search for Inanna, understand that I would personally find my way back into ordinary life by encountering a story from a culture that is now, itself, dead.

As I studied the Sumerian context and its gods, I found that Inanna invaded my imagination. Meeting her on her own terms, she helped me to gain language to understand what was happening within my own body-spirit-self. As I struggled to regain inner balance and wisdom after encountering a potentially life-threatening diagnosis, I actively sought to understand the antecedents of illness in my own life.

In working with the Inanna texts, I encountered a numinous presence whose origins lie in the mists of pre-history. I encountered a resurrection story of such power that it began to bring order out of the inner experiential chaos of my body, spirit, and psyche. Throughout this encounter, I was empowered to stay within an intense therapeutic process that resurrected and integrated body wisdom that had been dissociated within my personal life history.

Inanna's Story

What then is Inanna's own story? What do the recovered finds of archeologists tell us about her life and times? When we read the original sacred myths and poetry of Sumer, we find that Inanna's story teaches about the inevitability of suffering. We find that it also teaches about the amazing powers of faithful love to transform suffering into resurrection and renewed life.

In this Sumerian myth of death and resurrection, the goddess Inanna completed the cycle of life to which the underworld's voices called her. She traveled into the world of death. As she re-emerged from the land of death into the land of earth and sky, she returned to her role as goddess of the moon and the date palm oasis. By her return earth's fertility was once more assured and the cycle of the seasons was once again shaped into life's ongoing order and repetition. The moon returned to the sky and her star showed itself in the early evening or the early morning hours.

Personal Reflections

As I encountered Inanna's story with such immediacy, I began to find my own way back into life. My desire for full life emerged with such passion that I was simply unable to shape its internal gale force winds. At times I felt nearly shattered by the power of the life force as it flowed like an underground river throughout my days. In this encounter with life's own passion for my life, I became puzzled by its resurgence in my life at my life's midpoint. I asked myself, *to what purpose is this insistent desire to face life and to love life?*

Eventually, I decided that it was essential to my healing that I engage life on its own terms. I refused to stay embedded within relationships that negated the power of life. I understood the dangers of staying too closely tied to dysfunctional social systems that addictively seduced me to desire ongoing encounters with death and suffering.

Inanna's Story and Ruth's Story Merge

What follows, then, is my personal retelling of Inanna's story interpenetrated with my own story. Perhaps better said, it is the telling of my story now interpenetrated with wisdom from her story. I have tried to stay faithful to the structural narrative and intent of both stories. Where the Inanna of my poems wears jewelry, for example, it is the jewelry of the myth. Many of the metaphors of my own story are metaphors that I borrowed from the Sumerian mythologies. For example, the people of Sumer believed that the underworld was filled with dust and that the shades ate dust. Impaled upon the pole of the underworld, Inanna is, therefore, covered with and filled with dust.

Yet, I have felt free, as well, to bring contemporary images to my retelling of the myth. I have brought experiences, images and icons from my own life to the story. For example, I am fascinated by the ways in which so many Central American taverns often have a statue or picture of the Virgin of Guadalupe in the entryway to the bar. Seeing her there, I have often wondered who and what she protects.

In addition, I have introjected images and beliefs from other religious traditions than those of the Sumerian pantheon. In particular, I have utilized a religious perception or intuition from Semitic scriptures and traditions: knowing the name of a deity gives human beings powers over the deity. To know someone else's secret, sacred name means that her powers can be tamed, domesticated, channeled, or diverted. Thus, in my retelling, Inanna hears the voices calling her most secret names. Controlled by this esoteric knowledge of her true nature, she is, therefore, compelled to journey towards them.

To me this is a powerful metaphor of physical illness and of the soul's dark night. Someone or something knows our most intimate secret names. We are compelled to begin a journey of encounter with them even when we would prefer not to do so. Putting our own ear close to the ground, we hear emergent and nascent underworld intimations, intuitions, and voices. They insist we travel towards them in order to know them. Having heard them, we are bound to them. Being bound, we have already begun the journey to meet them and to know them.

In the poetry that follows, I seek to make sense out of Inanna's journey by thinking about issues and metaphors that surfaced to me in my own experience of an open body wound for twelve months. In re-reading Inanna's journey to the underworld, I repeatedly questioned her about her journey.

What must it have been like for a goddess to give up all of her divine powers to the power of death? What must it have felt like to lose sight of her star in the sky? What must it have meant to her to leave the stability of her chair of rule that was carved from the world tree? What did it mean to her to leave the comfort of the date palm oasis for a rugged journey into the underworld? What did she experience as she kept losing more and more of her garments, her jewelry, and her symbols of rule? What fears did she have? What doubts? What memories of other times?

In terms of the myth, I wanted to know what meanings were symbolized by items stripped from her at each gate. Were these only material items? Or, perhaps, were the material items a representation of much deeper spiritual and symbolic realities?

I wanted to know how she handled the loss of her powers. Certainly there must have been rage, terror, fear, grief, anxiety and an obsession with the consequences of her journey. Perhaps, I thought, she spent part of her journey through the seven gates of death by brooding over her life, asking herself questions about that which in her life had pleased her and that which had discomforted her. Perhaps, in turmoil and in confusion, she asked herself, "How did I get here?" Or, perhaps she asked herself, "How can I get out of here?" Maybe she even asked herself, "Why did I come here anyway?"

In addition, I sought to allow the ancient myth to enter dialogue with my own actual narrative of struggle and search. In particular, I began with therapeutic help to look at the questions raised by my post-surgical encounters with a disrupted and disorderly psyche and body. I began to search for deep acceptance and deep joy as the womb of my healing. At one point in the process I heard my clinician say, "When you can accept all of this body and psyche chaos as your teacher and be grateful to it, then life's own healing can begin to flow into your life, no matter what the specific outcome in your body." The inner resonance was so great that I knew this was truth. In my post-surgical encounters with physical wounds and weakness, I was guided to understand that I needed to seek healing for inner emotional and spiritual wounds as well.

Years later I look back from the land of the living into the world of physical trauma and emotional turmoil. I know that I have been taught much by Inanna's story and by my own life story. I continue to discover nuances to the teaching that our own wounds become great teachers for our continuing life. They can, I believe, become the source of even greater healing if we allow them to do so – bringing us to spiritual maturity and to a sense of equanimity that our lives have meaning even in the face of suffering.

I do not believe that life's goal for us is to celebrate our wounds. Rather, the necessity of our life is to integrate all of our experiences into a foundation for future life — the one we have lived along with the life that we are now seeking; I believe it will reveal its secrets to us if we will be quiet enough to listen.

One of our unique life tasks is to learn how to assimilate all aspects of our unique life journey as a teaching. We must learn how to search for life's lessons in a cyclical process that creates the inner matrix for transformation and resurrections.

The inner balance of destruction and creation; of death and resurrection; of lost stories and epiphanies; of losing and finding: this is a fragile balance. It shifts and moves and dances with us. When we learn to trust this inner balance, that which is most alive within us reaches towards and embraces life in all of its complexities. Our inward destructive and creative forces begin to work with each other in a new synthesis, in a new set of harmonies.

Slowly, day-by-day, I continue to assimilate awareness about acceptance and gratitude. Rereading the poetry itself, I can recognize moments of transforming metaphors. I can find the moments when a subtle shift from clutching pain and grief began. I find moments when a genuine celebration of being alive began to pulse in my veins like wild improvisational dancing. I found myself releasing fear, terror, rage, and despair. One of the most important metaphors from my therapeutic process was a teaching about celebrating breath itself – about allowing my self to be breathed by life and to find this current, present-moment breath to be sufficient.

Encountering Rachel Naomi Remen's Story

There was one more moment of healing synchronicity in which my spirit took another leap into understanding. Two years after my first surgery, my physical body was intact. The seroma had closed and it had closed well. I had had no major infection in a year of caring for an open wound. Medical care and therapeutic care had given me a renewed sense of personal competency in caring for my body and my self. I had, I thought, mastered the lessons. In these two years I had moved back into life.

I traveled to yet another professional meeting along the coasts of North Carolina. Physician-oncologist Rachel Naomi Remen was one of the speakers and she read from her book, *Kitchen Table Wisdom*. That morning she chose to read a short chapter in which she described her own personal encounter with primary intention healing many years ago. Hearing her written words spoken out loud helped me to find yet another set of concepts to use as help in understanding the reality and meaning of the body's ability to heal itself, even the major wounds.

No one had ever asked me to talk about the emotional or spiritual meaning of my seroma. I was aware of the intensity with which I had faced my wounded body. In the first month of the seroma's presence, I couldn't bear to look at it. Needing to take care of it had felt like an immense journey through terror. At times I simply broke down and cried over my appearance. I felt that my scarred post-surgery body had an evil and sinister appearance. For a while I called it Darth Vader. Then I decided to find an alternative image. I found a postcard of a Shar Pei dog and posted it on my mirror to remind me that my new post-surgical body was as wrinkled as a Shar Pei and as loyal to me as a favored pet. While I joked about this spontaneous imagery with my primary care physician and tried to find alternative images and metaphors, I was often overwhelmed by sadness at what had happened to my body. I felt deep pity for it.

As Remen described with eloquence, simplicity and humility her own response to a wound that needed to heal by its own internal guidance systems, her words brought me to a space of instantaneous, almost ecstatic, deep inner resonance. I began, on-the-spot, to have the courage to name my own uniquely personal responses to a post-surgical year of raw, chaotic confusion. I was, after all, alive. Why was this altered body so traumatic to me?

As I listened to her chapter reading, one which embedded within it the experience of continuous deep joy at being alive, I knew pockets of nearly untouchable (and certainly unsayable) grief and anger were there when I considered what had happened surgically to my body and spirit. Remen's matter-of-fact discussion of her own post-surgical encounter with fear and despair in a somewhat similar situation helped me begin to deal with the changes in my body's contours and appearance.

I wrote a letter to my therapist in the immediate hour after hearing her read. About my inner experience of this reading, I wrote:

> *She has given me a gift of life - a gift of knowing that I am not totally alone in the world. She has traveled a similar road and made it through. Somewhere in the forest of my feelings about cancer, surgery, and seroma; somewhere in the wilderness of my feelings about surgeons, hospitals, medical insurance and curing systems; somewhere in the psychic wounding of this physical wounding, there is a path for me to find and to walk. I know there is a path because she has just named it. Just as I knew there was an interstate highway between Chicago and Berkeley before I drove it, I now know there is a path to integrating this wound into my life and being stronger for that work. But just now, these emotions of healing are so new, so raw, so ragged, I cannot name them. Right now they are simply shattering something deep within and they are reshaping it. That which was inchoate within the death fantasies and the experience of being physically wounded for a full year is being illumined.*

None of us know who will touch us with healing or who, in turn, we will touch. In the world of books and professional meetings, I encountered two healers who touched my life even though they had no idea of my name or my life situation. Both wrote in published books about their own struggles as healers and as women. Both brought me the gift of life. One (Dr. Bolen) introduced me to Inanna and her descent into the underworld. Two years later, the second (Dr. Remen) told me about her own responses after abdominal surgery to the awesome need for the body to be the body's own healer. In a very real sense these two physicians, Dr. Bolen and Dr. Remen, who had never heard my story and who do not know me, became part of a healing network for my body and my spirit. My gratitude to both is deep and flowing.

Healing Promises

As part of my inner dialogue with this teaching about breath and the flow of healing, there was a specific day when I promised an inner soft voice that "I can and will bear witness to life and its healing powers among us and within us. Finding healing and joy returning to my inner life, I will try to speak my understandings of its truth in the ordinary world."

Therefore, I now bring my journey and Inanna's journey to you as a witness to the power of life over death; as a teaching about metamorphosis, transformation and resurrection; as a gift to those whose healing presence has flowed into and through my life; as a reminder to us all that there may be many cycles through death in a lifetime. Each cycle teaches us about life's depths if we are willing to accept the teaching.

Therefore, I created and now bring forth this poetry as an offering.

The poetry of this book speaks about one individual's encounters with the Sumerian goddess Inanna. As you read this contemporary re-telling of an early ancient Near Eastern myth, listen to it with an open heart. Accept it for what it is – one woman's story of healing of the physical body, the energetic body, the historical body, and the guiding spirit we call Life.

THE DEATH MASKS

In addition to working with a medical therapist skilled in hypnotic body/mind therapy, two therapeutic activities during my year of caring for my abdominal seroma contributed much to my understanding of Inanna's journey into the underworld.

Within the context of working in body-mind therapy with hypnotically-recalled dissociated material, I often found myself in the position of having no ability to describe in rational, linear speech the experiences I was having. I had no language to discuss recalled memories – many of which were kinesthetic. In the therapeutic meeting, I discovered that I was literally speechless about my inner world. Every evening I began to write what I knew and what I was learning. The writing hand knew truths and vocabularies that the speaking mouth could not allow itself to speak.

As I began to re-exercise my writing muscles, the poetry in this volume erupted first. Hearing the therapist explain clinically dissociated materials in terms of a "missing shadow tree" I wrote a poem to explore my own understanding of shadow trees.

After hearing Bolen's lecture and after reading her book (*Close to the Bone)*, I found snatches of my journey expressed in the ideas of Inanna's journey. After I'd re-read Inanna's mythic story of chthonic descent, I began to read Jungian clinical literature on archetypal meaning. In the synchronistic interface between the mythic story of Inanna's own descent into the underworld of death and suffering and my own very real personal world of having a post-surgical open body wound to deal with, symbolic imagery emerged into my awareness by means of poetry.

In addition, I began to deliberately construct and use imagery as part of the healing process. I read theory books about guided imagery and healing. Years before in a Canadian workshop led by Frank Lawliss and Jean Achteberg, I had met a magical dolphin and had made a truly inspiring journey on the dolphin's back to a magical island of women healers. Even before that, in graduate school, Jeannette Rainwater had introduced me to wise old woman in the attic imagery and I had been impressed with its power to inform me.

Healing imagery, poetic imagery, information about the goddess Inanna, hypnotic recall and therapeutically-guided imagery: all of this intense psychological work seemed to open doors deep inside the self. Inside these doors, I found my life history to be stored. Much of it was expressed in kinesthetic knowing and in imagistic knowing.

As I worked with the poetry, some phrases in Spanish seemed more appropriate to me than words in English. When I'd first lived in a second nation outside my homeland, I was able to read the language but was not fluently able to speak it or to readily understand others who were speaking it. In the fourteen months I lived as an expatriate in a Spanish-speaking world, I had the experience of being surrounded by incomprehensible words and customs. I was an eager learner as I sought to find my way in a totally new life situation – a place where I was the cultural outsider. During those months abroad, I had learned how to rely on my personal powers of observation in order to understand at least some of the realities that surrounded me.

After the seroma opened and I worked with medical caregivers and body healers to find my body's own pathway back into wholeness, imagistic metaphors for living in the strange land of illness with a slowly healing body emerged – sometimes in Spanish and sometimes in English. I would sometimes hear my inner noisy mind's dialogue with itself and catch a phrase of Spanish that seemed to capture my emotional state better than any equivalent phrase in English. It seemed to me as if my body-self-mind was utilizing my previous experience of learning how to successfully and happily live in a foreign land with unique and strange customs as a map for learning how to cooperate with my body's healing processes in the strange land I now inhabited – with a wounded body that needed to heal by its own efforts. Every day I sought ways to understand and to cooperate with the body's own wisdom about healing itself.

Emmett's Question

One day my therapist said to me, *do you do any art work? You are having such trouble expressing yourself in language. I wonder if painting might be useful to you.* The suggestion seemed very timely and I immediately set myself to making masks. For years, in my professional career as a college teacher, I'd taught successive generations of students how to make masks as one way of learning about themselves and others. I'd witnessed the power of mask work to reveal deeper truths even as it appeared to hide away the face.

During my year-long academic sabbatical leave of absence I lived in a small Berkeley apartment that had an outdoor overhang. The area was secluded from the street. I set up a table with all of the equipment that I needed. Only two of my closest neighbors became aware of what I was doing as each morning I emerged with my *art equipment.* For more than six months, I spent an hour or two each morning in mask work. After a mask was completed, I carried it, in turn, to three separate clinical offices. My two physicians and my Upledger body worker would seek to understand that experience which I could not yet speak, that inner sensory and kinesthetic experience which was almost totally disconnected (dissociated from language).

The first masks (#One: My Life Changed; #Two, The Shadow Tree, #Three, Hearing Voices from Below; #Four, The Shattered Face; #Five, Split Apart and Separated), dealt with an old car accident nearly thirty years before. For the first hours after this accident I had no memory and no recall. It was in the hypnotic trance that the hours inside the car, the ambulance, and the emergency room could re-enter awareness. For more than two years after their first appearance in hypnotic trance, sensory memories slowly returned. As sensory and kinesthetic memory (that which I began to call body memory or felt sense memory) returned, I found more and more narrative memory returning as well.

Near death then, I'd fought to regain life. In the immediate aftermath of the accident, I put all of my energy into regaining my life. I had dental repair work done. I had physical therapy for painful muscles. I drove my car on back mountain roads when I needed to stop every ten or fifteen minutes to cry and deal with intense anxiety as other cars drove towards me. I spent time with my friend, the driver of the accident car, who'd had cranial-spinal cord injuries and who needed repeated neurological surgeries in order to heal herself. I made decisions about suing the drunk driver who had plowed into our car at full speed. I pushed my lawyer to tell the sentencing judge that I wanted the drunk driver in jail. I bent my young and prodigious life energy to the only goal I could have: I was intent on regaining my life. I was determined that I was not going to be permanently victimized by a drunk driver.

The only psychological remnant that remained was severe anxiety at driving on rainy nights or on Friday evenings. Because I understood these were remnants, I rearranged my life to control the anxiety. If I was a passenger in a car on rainy, dark nights, I taught myself to fall asleep instantly so I didn't have to see the on-coming lights shattered by raindrops. If I was driving, I either stopped driving or drove very cautiously. In general, during the drinking hours on Friday evening, I did not drive.

In all of my journals and therapy work, I referred to these masks as the death mask series. As I began to work with the masks, I evolved an understanding of these masks that was fairly primitive. Some of the masks were constructed to reveal an inner experience for which I had absolutely no language. For example, the yellow

Shattered Face mask was a deliberate attempt to show my physician and my Upledger body worker what my face felt like inside the hypnotic state of consciousness when I was hypnotically living at the site of a life-threatening car accident in chronologically distant but hypnotically present time.

Later masks dealt with issues of family violence when I was a small child (#Six, The Watcher; #Seven, The Red Whore; #Eight, The Guardians). I had always remembered specific events of maternal violence – in a sense, the content of the issues. What I'd dissociated from ordinary consciousness were the child's fear, terror, confusion, and enraged anger. After therapeutic sessions in which I'd been absolutely unable to describe what had been uncovered in my inner life, I talked with my siblings who confirmed for me that my memories were accurate and that I was not crazy.

Eventually, I learned to name the specifics out loud. The day I first spoke in concrete words, specific details of a particular beating I'd kept alive as a mantra in childhood (*I won't forget this day and you can kill me but you cannot make me cry*), the look of horror on my therapist's face startled me. Before this appointment, I had never captured that this particular form of "spanking" had been unacceptable adult parental behavior towards me, a child. I began to understand dissociated clinical material from the inside out. I remembered the facts of what had happened but I had absolutely no awareness of anything else related to the beating. In hypnotic recall, the terror and rage re-emerged along with my dogged insistence to myself that I would survive her and I would not forget.

During this time the masks worked with revealing that which was concealed in such a way that the front of the mask participated in hiding personal experience while the reverse image of the mask was more revelatory. For example, the mask *Chaos Creates Transformation* was created in the middle of therapeutic work oriented around reclaiming body-memories from childhood's maternal beating and face-slapping behaviors.

This particular mask was one of the turning points in the therapeutic process. One evening as I was at dinner, I said to myself, *I will destroy the mask I am now working on*. When I got home from the restaurant, I got out a cutting board, a large hammer, and a partially-created mask. I began hammering the mask with such intensity that the cutting board shattered. I kept on hammering the mask and the board (fully aware of my rage) into smaller and smaller pieces. The tubular holder of this particular mask represents a whole shadow forest of emotions. The now limp and faceless mask with no recognizable features for the viewer is tied onto the tube. At the base of the mask, I glued on several of the shards of the cutting board. I kept working on this mask for several more days. One night, as I worked on the mask, I spontaneously decided to use one of the little dolls from my childhood's stash to represent an image of inner transformation taking place inside of me as the earlier child was finally able to begin to deal with the terror and rage of being beaten by an out-of-control mother, as the child was finally able to tell herself the truth of her own childhood.

As a well-seasoned therapist in my clinical self, I was simply amazed that these issues emerged around a wounded mid-life body that was actually healing itself in an orderly way. I was having no infections. The seroma was, my primary care doctor told me, healing in ordinary and measurable ways. My psyche seemed more unruly.

As a formally trained clinician in therapy, I not only utilized my therapist as my helper. I read every book and article I could find that described dissociative phenomena. I talked with some of my clinical teachers and friends who were therapists. Once again I was insistent that I would regain my life and that it would be a rich, full, committed, passionate life.

As I worked, studied and talked with my clinical friends, I realized that I had never before spoken of these issues to anyone. My closest friends spontaneously began to make a repeating comment, *Ruth, I never knew about your car accident. Ruth, I never knew about your childhood abuse. Ruth I never knew*. I realized that while I had kept the memory of the facts of what had happened alive and while I never had doubted that my memories had happened, I simply had discounted the importance of the event.

I knew the car accident had permanently changed my life just as I knew the cancer surgery and its aftermath had done the same. I knew the diagnosis of macular degeneration (gradual blurred vision) was already beginning to shape my ongoing life and work. I just didn't think anybody would care enough about me to want to hear about my complex search for a reasonable narrative and a path to integration and wholeness.

Hearing the loving concern of my friends as we chatted by telephone, I became internally committed to learning how to share important internal events with my friends. I decided that, narcissistic or not, I would show my family, my closest personal friends, and my professional colleagues two things: the death mask series and the poetry that I'd begun to call *Inanna's Way.*

Somewhere during this time I ordered *Warming the Stone Child* audio-tape. In this tape Clarisa Estes Pinkola discusses a Jungian perspective on pre-verbal children and mid-childhood children who lived with abuse and violence. I re-read Alice Miller's book, *The Drama of the Gifted Child: The Search for the True Self.* I found Wayne Muller's book, *Legacy of the Heart: The Spiritual Advantage of a Painful Childhood.* As I worked in body-mind therapy to re-conceptualize my life's experiences, I became willing – and empowered -- to work with the terror. I grew able to name it out loud to a few selected individuals.

As I grew more and more secure in re-claiming my personal and familial history, I said to myself, *I refuse to be victimized by this very personal history of maternal abusiveness. I refuse to be victimized by an old car accident. In short, I refuse to claim a personal identity of victim.* Within my birth-family and with my closest friends, there were conversations of confirmation and affirmation. My closest friends supported my decision to move slowly in talking with other people about my life history.

Although there were days when my world seemed very chaotic and regressed, I knew, experientially, that I was not crazy. I also knew it was my choice about how widely I talked about my personal experiences with life-changing trauma. I knew that it was my decision to make if I decided to tell my personal story in a more public context.

Later some of the masks became more deliberately related to more intellectual aspects of the therapy process. For example, the mask, *Inanna: Queen of Heaven* was created as I was beginning to feel and find my way out of the psychic underworld of trauma and suffering. This is also a mask in which the face has been hammered into a limp, torn flat surface. When the physical mask was almost totally destroyed, I took all of the inherited threads out of my dead mother's sewing box and began to stitch them onto the mask where I began to braid them.

As a child I had worn braids and I had always hated them. But my mother would never allow me to cut my hair nor to let it flow free in the breezes. My braids had been a source of much contentious behavior between the two of us. As I worked with my mother's threads, I began to see how beautiful these thread braids could be. As I worked with each braid I tried to make the collection of threads into something lovely – something that truly masked the shattered plaster mask into which the threads were being sewn.

Poetry and masks now came with one breath. I was writing and I was creating masks. The masks became the pathway to speaking the unspeakable. They became the gate to transmuting unbelievable anxiety, rage, and self-doubt into believable words. They also became the gift of playful, creative joy.

The poetry became a way of externalizing that which was internal. I needed to search for metaphors that could carry the intensity of the inner experience. The written poetry became the gateway to words. Once something was written, I became more able to talk about it within spontaneous therapeutic conversation. The more I encoded kinesthetic and sensory experience into language, the more I felt myself gaining mastery and competency with my life's narrative.

The final masks in the death mask series were a deliberate effort to deal with Inanna's historical mythology in representational space. I read about the stars and Sumerian astrology. I read about the iconic animals that represent Inanna and her immense powers. I studied the myth's structure in light of today's chakra theory. I examined the colors of goddess representation. I read other sections of Sumer's ancient mythology to gain a better sense of her complexity and role in Sumerian life. I thought about shamanic healing.

Each of the masks has a revealing aspect. However, each mask in this series also has much that is hidden. I enjoyed opening up a visual reality that expressed the wordless. I also enjoyed playing with that which was open. Often, I painted it over in an obsessive process of uncovering and covering. At some level I knew I was "messing with my mind" and also "with the mind of my therapist." At times I reminded him that *great art should never be explained but only experienced.* At others, it was very important to me that he understand exactly what had happened during the construction of a mask.

Unearthing and revealing; covering over and re-hiding; transmutation and transformation of that which was often unbearable to speak: it was these internalized dialogue processes that drove the poetry-mask-making experiment.

Even though some times it felt like play, I kept track of what I was doing with a camera. The layers of each mask were represented in a photographic history. I didn't want to lose the hard-won insights that had emerged during each mask's creation.

Reflecting much study as well as much personal musing about gods and goddesses, I more deliberately and painstakingly created the last set of masks in the death mask series. They were much more intellectual constructions than were the first ones. For example, the mask, *Inanna, Queen of Earth* utilized rich sea-colored paper with gold embossing. It also utilized sea shells which I'd collected in tropical oceans while I lived in Central America. It was a mask intended to reflect an image of the goddess as she resumed her rule in ordering all matters of earth's capacity to provide bounty for human beings.

There is a sense in which one must look at the masks to understand the poetry. But the reverse is equally true. To understand the masks, one must absorb the meaning of the poetry. Each mode of expression arose in this time of almost total speechlessness and muteness about my inner world. When, in a healer's office, I could not say out loud what needed to be said for information to be transmitted or for the healer's understanding to occur, I could write and I could sculpt masks on my face.

In my search for healing, I had no intention of smashing my own physical face as a way to uncover memory. But I had no trouble slashing and smashing the plaster masks. I had no intention of harming myself in any way. But when I felt it was needed to express my inner rage, I felt quite free to assault a mask with hammers, knives and scissors.

I could verbally speak. I had no trouble using the physical voice. But when it came to telling the forbidden family stories of violence and the stories of accidental, out-of-consciousness, out-of body terror – then I simply could not find my way into speech at all. I was mute. Towards the end of my therapy, the therapist said something like this to me, *for many, many weeks at the beginning of our relationship, this process felt very tenuous to me. As you would leave my office, I would wonder whether you would return or not. You seemed so very unsure of yourself and of your work with me.*

The process never felt tenuous to me. I had made a commitment to myself to do the work. I lined up a cadre of friends and former teachers who listened without judgment and were the guardians of my safety. I said to each of them, *if you sense that I am in active psychological danger, I want you to tell me. Otherwise, I am going to do this even though I am terrified of hypnotic therapy methodologies. You are my guardians. I want you to look after my well-being so that I don't have to.* This meant, then, that I was committed to telling each of these friends what was happening inside the therapy hour. I decided to myself that I would have no secrets in what I discovered or didn't discover.

Concerned that my body had needed two surgeries and that the second surgery had resulted in a huge open abdominal wound, I felt that the psychological risk of a therapeutic journey through internal chaos was more important than the safety of not knowing the roots of illness and distress that was already present in my life. I was as determined as I have ever been to learn what had led my body into such a specificity of wounds.

In addition, hoping I might be able to arrest my continuing progression towards blindness, I wanted to learn what I could learn about what had happened to my psyche to create such inner terrors that I was frequently mute for minutes at a time. I wondered about the connection of maternal violence to muteness and to the activation of a familial eye disease. I wondered what role old car accidents played in the biological processes of macular degeneration.

Caught in long moments of absolute muteness, I knew I didn't have words in these moments because I had no comprehensible thoughts. All I had was the experience of raw terror or the emotion of pure rage to serve as my guides. I was not refusing to tell my therapist what I was experiencing. I had absolutely no language to express it. I was like a pre-verbal child inside the therapy hour. All I had were kinesthetic sensations and sensory awareness to guide me.

The masks and written journals and poetry had to carry the story line for many, many weeks and months as I sought to re-member and re-create an inner balance and joy in my life. The death masks, along with the poetry that accompanied them, became, in my personal reality, life masks. Externalizing the wordless and inchoate into concrete material forms allowed me to step back from the internal struggle to encode my personal experience in language. In the creative process of destruction and creation, I found many metaphors for my inner life.

Interestingly enough, one of the things I eventually found in more than three years of focused mask making was a sense of play. I began to tease my terrors and play with my angers. I began to have active conversations with them as I asked them to show me how they wanted to be represented by color and form. In a kind of mystical sense-making, I welcomed them home as my teachers and playmates. They began to be my friends. They became important guides in finding the path through the shadow tree forest.

When a mask was completed, I knew. I was never in any doubt about when a mask was finished – when it spoke what it needed to speak. I often felt as if the mask itself guided the mask's creation.

On some of the masks, which had been born in emotional states of great anxieties and nearly overwhelming angers, I deliberately planted some small symbol of hope or transformation. It may have been hidden under layers of paper and paint or it may have been planted on the face of the mask for immediate visibility. I became attached to the idea of including iconic symbols of totemic spirits as guardians and protectors. For example, the mask *Picasso Face* was the first mask to deal explicitly with maternal violence. When the mask was finished, I found monarch butterfly seals in a stationery store. I carefully pasted thirteen of these seals on the face of the mask. I was seeking transformation and felt that butterflies were a wonderful iconic representation of metamorphosis and transformation.

Even in the midst of emotional and physical turmoil, I insisted upon hope, joy and personal contentment as my birthright. I was prepared to work long and hard to re-find it.

That the mask work brought such pleasure was an unexpected benefit. Each completed mask hinted at additional masks that waited to be made. Once or twice I was so impatient to learn what a given mask could teach me, I would work on two separate ones at the same time. But usually, I was focused on one mask at a time.

I dreamed masks; I read about masks; I studied masks; I visited museum masks. I began to understand the mythical and archetypal language of masking. In that visual, unspoken understanding of masking and revealing, healing language and experience were both born.

ANCIENT SUMER'S INANNA

Who was Inanna and what was her journey? What we know about her has been brought into our contemporary era as scholars have located and translated Sumer's clay cuneiform tablets recovered from today's landmass of Iraq. Thousands of years ago, her priests, priestesses and scribes carved stories about Inanna and her place within Sumer's cosmology. They left them behind as Sumer's power waned and Inanna's temples were abandoned.

The mythic Inanna was a goddess. In her own era she was the most powerful deity in the Sumerian pantheon. Her story, according to Pritchard (1961), sheds light on Sumero-Babylonian religious beliefs. Worship of her was born in prehistory and her lineage can only be guessed at. As with many succeeding goddesses, she appears to have appropriated powers and symbols of lesser deities into her own.

Sumer was to its era what Greece was to its era. Sumer's influence followed the trade routes and it is believed by some historians that evidences of Inanna's influence and importance can be found as far west as England and as far east as India and China. As century followed century her names as a dominating goddess changed just as political powers changed and empires changed. Because of her many names and her many iconic representations as, for example, the Queen of Heaven, today's scholars trace her to

Aphrodite/Venus in the Greco-Roman centuries. In addition, many of her iconic and representative symbols have become associated with Christianity's Virgin Mary (Baring and Cashford, 1991).

Worship centers for the cult of Inanna/Ishtar occurred within two different ethnic groups. In the south, in Sumer, the goddess was called Inanna. Stories about her from this place were centered in temples in Sumer's major cities. To the north, the Semitic people known as the Akkadians called their leading goddess Ishtar. Many of Inanna's attributes and iconic symbols were taken over by Ishtar.

The particular myth that I have chosen to use is known as *the Sumerian Descent of Inanna.* In the Sumerian story, the goddess sets her heart upon going to the underworld. At each of the underworld's seven gates she requests entrance.

A similar myth, yet one which is nuanced somewhat differently, appears later in history as *the Akkadian Descent of Ishtar*. The two descent stories represent somewhat different perspectives on Inanna's personality. In the Akkadian story she is bolder in her behaviors at the underworld's gate. In this version she pounds on the door to the underworld and demands entrance.

In my re-telling of the Inanna myth, I have chosen to stay within the constraints of the earlier Sumerian version while remaining aware of the later Akkadian one.

In *The Descent of Inanna,* the clay tablets describe the journey of Inanna from her home in the heavens where she rules as daughter of the moon and queen of the date palm oasis. She decides to journey into the underworld domain ruled by her older sister, Ereshkigal. Her reasons for making this journey are unknown to us.

In Sumer's stories about Ereshkigal, we learn that she lived in a lapis lazuli palace in the middle of a great underworld cave where the shades lived in darkness and were covered with dust. The relationship of the two sisters is not explained in great detail.

Pritchard (1961) raises the question of whether Ereshkigal was Inanna's enemy.

The clay tablets tell us that when she heard the voices of the underworld, Inanna immediately dressed in the regal garments of her rule as goddess of the sky and earth. In the extant text that we have, however, it appears as if she had a premonition that not all would go well during her journey. Before she began her journey, she advised her loyal servant Ninshubar to watch for her return. She warned Ninshubar that she might not be able to leave the underworld in order to return to earth by a certain time and requested that Ninshubar contact the gods and ask them to search for her and rescue her.

Leaving Ninshubar behind, she traveled towards the underworld. Arriving at the entrance to Ereshkigal's realm, she had to pass seven gates or thresholds and meet the demands of seven gate guardians. At each gate she was forced by that gate's guardian to give away a garment, a piece of jewelry, or some other valued sign of her rule as queen of the upper worlds.

Arriving at the seventh gate, she was stripped of all remaining garments, jewelry and signs of her rule. She was forced to crawl naked into Ereshkigal's presence. Here Ereshkigal was joined by the Anunnaki, the seven dreaded judges of Sumer's underworld.

Her elder sister was not happy to see Inanna and fixed on her the eyes of death. Turned into a corpse, Inanna was hung on the peg of death like a slab of decaying meat. For three days and three nights (the nights of the dark moon) she hung there.

When Inanna did not return on time, her servant Ninshubar asked various Sumerian gods for help. Each God refused to change the rules of the realm of death except Enki, the god of wisdom. To help Inanna return to life, Enki created small genderless creatures that crept into the underworld. Their only mission was to rescue Inanna. As instructed by Enki, they sprinkled on her the food and waters of life. Following this sprinkling, Inanna was returned to full life.

Faced with her now reborn and living sister, Ereshkigal agreed that Inanna might return to the upper world of earth and sky. However, she insisted that the rules of the realm of death must still be followed. A substitute needed to be brought back to the realm of death.

As she traveled home, Inanna refused to condemn her faithful mourning servants to take her place. She refused to condemn her mourning children.

However, as she came to her place of rule she found her lover-consort Dumuzi sitting in the place of rule. He was sitting in a chair carved out of the world tree. He was not mourning her absence. Inanna immediately gave Dumuzi to Ereshkigal's demons so that they could carry him back to the underworld in her place.

She then resumed her rule.

RESOURCES CONSULTED

Baring, A. and Cashford, J. (1991). *The Myth of the Goddess: Evolution of an Image.* London, UK: Arkana/Penguin.

Kramer, S. N. (1967). *Cradle of a Civilization.* NY: Time-Life Books; (1961). *History Begins at Sumer.* London, UK: Thames and Hudson; (1994). *Sumerian Mythology* (Philadelphia: American Philosophical Society Memoirs, Volume 27, pp. 89-93; (1989). *Myth of Enki: The Crafty God.* New York, NY: Oxford, 1989.

Kramer, S. N., Ed. (1961). *Mythologies of the Ancient World* Garden City, NJ: Doubleday, pp. 93-137.

Wolkstein, D. and Kramer, S. N. (1983). *Inanna: Queen of Heaven and Earth: Her Stories and Hymns.* New York, NY: Harper and Row.

Pritchard, J. B. (Ed.). (1961). *Ancient Near Eastern Texts Relating to the Old Testament, 3rd edition with Supplement.* Princeton, NJ: Princeton University Press.

A JUNGIAN ANALYSIS

Some of today's Jungian theorists (Bolen, 1996, Perera, 1981) raise the possibility that Ereshkigal and Inanna were two aspects of the same deity in Sumerian understanding. This was a common feature in later mythologies about female deities that emerge in the Mediterranean basin (Walker, 1983).

In a contemporary Jungian (and therapeutic) hermeneutic, the dual aspect of Inanna-Ereshkigal represents one deity. In the aspect of Ereshkigal, the goddess represents the denied self; the dissociated or abandoned self; the wounded self who has been refused expression. Thus denied, she rages in the underground of the personality. In any life crisis, such as a life-threatening illness, her demands must be confronted for the life force to continue the needed processes of death and transformation.

In her book, *Close to the Bone: Life Threatening Illness and the Search for Meaning,* Jean Shinoda Bolen (1996) has written about the ability of *Inanna's Descent* story to illuminate the journey of today's individuals, particularly women, into and beyond today's terrifying and life-threatening illnesses such as breast cancer:

> Metaphorically and actually, illness and hospitalization strip us of what covered and protected us in many ways…the journey is similar to Inanna's. There are still gates we go through which

> strip us of persona and defense: we become exposed and bare-souled. The stripping away makes it possible for us to reach depths within ourselves that we might otherwise not reach. (31-32)

In these depths, Bolen speculates, we encounter whatever we have buried or abandoned or forgot about ourselves. These repressed and denied aspects of our selves lie in waiting. They suffer the pain and rage of not being fully integrated into our adult consciousness.

This Jungian, feminist perspective was helpful to me as I began to work with the *Descent of Inanna* and the *Descent of Ishtar* narratives as a way to deal with my own unexpected, mid-life encounter with uterine cancer. As I sought to recapture and understand formerly dissociated aspects of my own personality, I found hope in the story of the divine underworld journey of death and resurrection.

Many writers in the field of cancer studies comment that a malignancy provides certain individuals with an opportunity for personal choices and growth. In facing the possibility of bodily mutilation or death, the individual confronts issues that are not an ordinary part of routine adult life. Needing to confront a potentially life-threatening diagnosis and a forever-changed physical body, a certain clarity emerges within the personality around issues of importance and issues of meaning. For many cancer survivors, the experiences of illness and treatment provide the mandate for deep, inner reflection. Understanding that life, and the quality of life, are treasured in new ways, these individuals radically begin to reshape their sense of themselves and the world.

REFERENCES CONSULTED

Women Healers Encounter Inanna

Bolen, J. S. (1994). *Crossing to Avalon: A Woman's Midlife Pilgrimage.* San Francisco, CA Harper and Row.

Bolen, J. S. (1996). *Close to the Bone: Life-Threatening Illness and the Search for Meaning.* New York, NY: Scribners.

Reis, P. (1991). *Through the Goddess: A Woman's Way of Healing.* New York, NY: Continuum.

Perera, S. (1981). *Descent to the Goddess: A Way of Initiation for Women.* Toronto, Canada: Inner City Books.

Walker, B.G. (1988). *The Woman's Dictionary of Symbols and Sacred Objects.* San Francisco, CA: Harper and Row.

Walker, B. G. (1983). *The Woman's Encyclopedia of Myths and Secrets.* San Francisco, CA: Harper and Row.

Weiner, S. with H. Smith (Fall, 1994/Winter, 1995) A Tale of Two Sisters (pp. 8-10) in *Ways of the Healer.* San Francisco, CA: Program of Medicine and Philosophy, California Pacific Medical Center.

THE POETRY

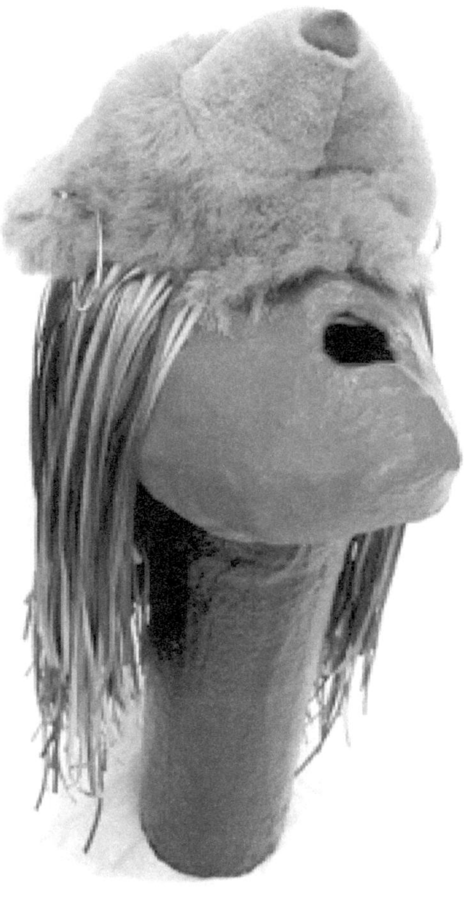

THE HOMELAND - CRUZANDO LA FRONTERA

MY LIFE CHANGED

Earth I am
Fire I am
Water, Air, and Spirit I am[1]

The morning and the evening star are mine
Lions sit at peace with me in secluded courtyards
Dolphins pull my chariot in the sacred pools
Thunder and lightning speak my will

I am Inanna!
I am the moon's daughter!
I am the queen of heaven!

1. Chant taught by Mathew Fox, "Body and Soul Conference," Seattle, WA, Spring 1996.

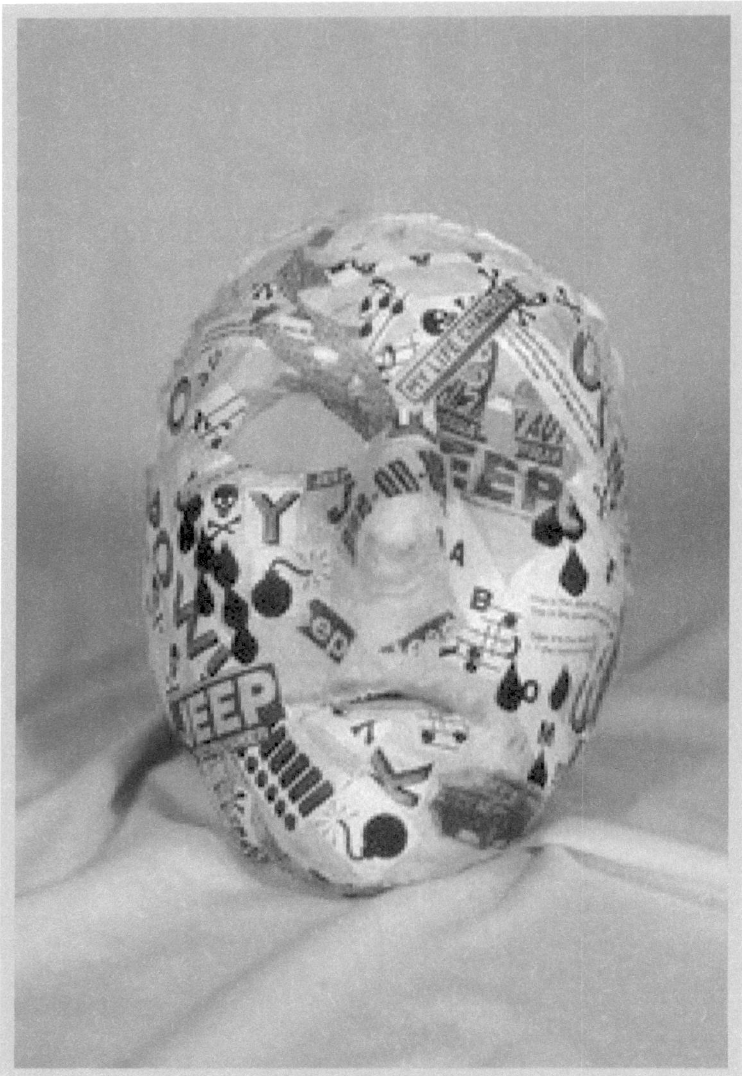

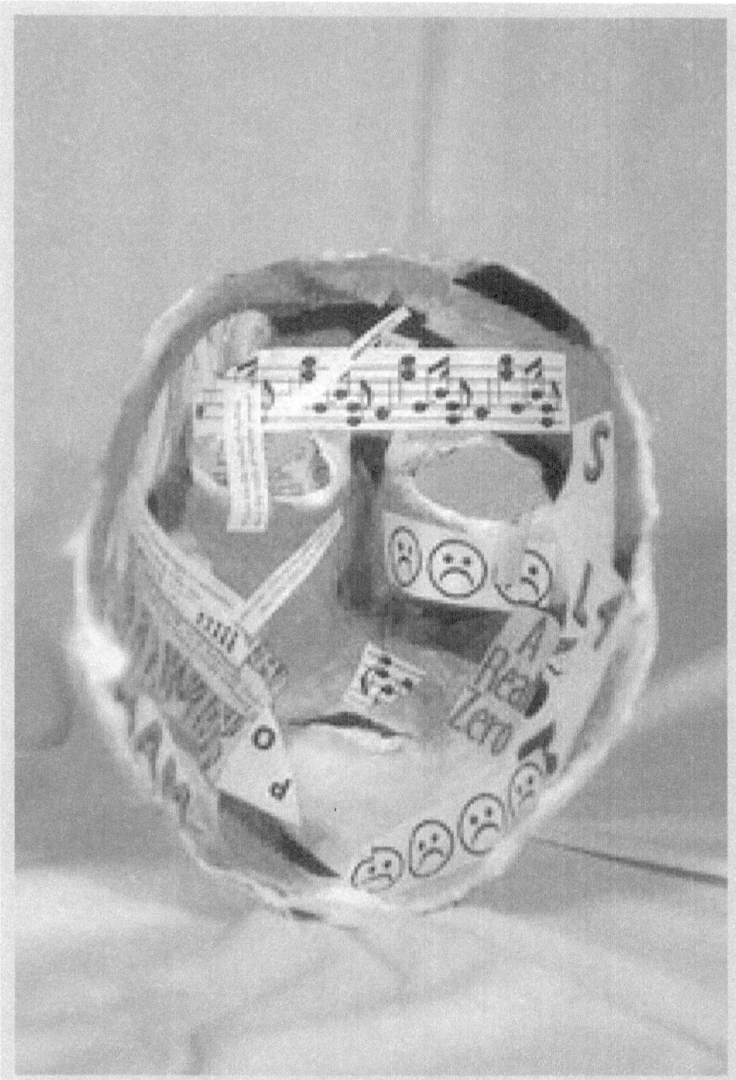

El árbol sagrado del mundo

Root hairs of the huluppu tree reach deep into sweet-smelling mud
And sense no separation of water, root and ground.
One with all it surrounds
The huluppu tree is surrounded by all.
In oneness the huluppu tree sinks its roots deep into river's fertile soil
And knows itself to be river mud and water as well as huluppu tree.

Los remolinos móviles de arena

By morning the moon's receding light
Slips noiselessly across dawn's emerging sky.
Drugged with sleep I watch shadowy forms dance
Inside locked doors and across shuttered windows.
Aroused by their entry into this lonely sleeping room
I worry these sleep-encrusted musings
Conceal dense truths
By obscuring them inside my thorn-covered thickets of reverie.
Circling close within the musings of this sleepy place
My mind's sand tornadoes whirl and whisper
Seductive echoes of knowing within unknowing.
Spinning and twisting across the sandpapered world of morning
Dust demons hiss vile rumors
So faint and so distant
I pray myself safe from their foul, damaging breaths.

Una canción pequeña para el viaje

Searching for horizon's stillpoint
I hear inner song-calls.
They draw my spirit to the living riverway
From whose blood-red clay
The first tree grows.

Under moon's descending crescent

I purify this wounded body in a pool of troubled waters.
I mark my face with sacred ochre.
I dance naked in the rain and wind.
I wait but know not why I wait.

Una frontera oscura

Yesterday I crossed borders
But knew not how I passed from one land into the second.

There were no border guards
With guns at the ready to prevent my passing.
There were no petty functionaries
With stamps and inks to mark my papers
Or to deny my travel rights.
There were no gates to seal the boundaries
To foreigners and aliens – all those who do not belong.
There were no trained dogs with bared teeth
To stop me from straying.

Yesterday I crossed borders
But knew not how I passed from one land into the second.

Hace muchos años

Under unlit skies I packed a quick bag.
I filled it with all my necessities.
I rolled up laughter like underpants and tucked it into the bag's corners.
I folded grief's tears into neat squares.
I wrapped rage in tissue paper so it wouldn't wrinkle.
I poured terror into leak-proof bottles.
I tucked happiness into mesh bags so it wouldn't mold.
I stuffed curiosity into the bag's side pockets along with a new toothbrush.

Standing in front of my mirror
I made womanly oblations to the future.

I twined my hair in a purple turban covered with sparkling gemstones.
I placed silver and quartz pendants in my ears.
I covered my neck with gold, lapis, and turquoise.
I protected my heart with chains of copper mesh and emeralds.
I wove a belt of amber beads and tied it securely around my hips.
I wrapped coral bracelets around my wrists and ankles.
I secured a soft, wooly breechcloth with two clasps of bloodstone.

Empieza el viaje

I clutch my bag of treasures
And walk blind under black clouds thick with storm warnings.
Under my outer robe, embraced close to my breastskin,
I hug sacred manuscripts.
Illumined with gold leaf and powdered gem calligraphy.
These hoarded scrolls have lured me to this strange enchanted land
With its rumbling river, its first tree, its song-calls.

In trance, I walk barefooted across the sand hills.
I do not feel the pain of the sun's embedded heat
Nor the chill of the night wind.

El vendaval del norte

Having begun this journey
In search of whatever wisdom can be found
By journeying,
I mark the hurricane's blow that batters my face.
Hailstones beat upon my head.
They open wounds so savage
I think I cannot move.

I drop my bag on the ground
To crouch low over its lock.

What is the treasure contained within
That has brought down the sky's wrath?
What gods have I so offended
They have turned their faces away from mine?
Why have they left me abandoned in this strange place
Whose borders I have so innocently transgressed?
Where were their border guards?
Where were their warning signs?
Where were their locked gates with snarling guard dogs?
Why were there no signs to mark the frontiers of a land
Where hurricane gales blow constantly
And rain slashes unto my already wet cheeks?

In this storm, why was the border not closed
So that all passersby might avoid the raging, swollen river
Where the first tree grows its roots in blood-red soil?

Raíz dulce
Marking my naked belly with tattooed spirals,
I begin to dance with towering winds.
Tormented by strange sounds and desires
I whirl in this erratic night.

I am surrounded by the storm
Just as I surround the storm.

I am the storm.

Una canción encantadora de la noche
I grow by the riverbank
And sink my roothairs deep into blood-red clay.
I am become huluppu tree.

My roothairs reach deep into the sweet-smelling mud.
I am become tree, mud and sacred river.

ON ENTERING THE DARK WOODS

Sounds I cannot hear call me
Sights I cannot see lure me
Tastes I cannot taste tempt me
Aromas I cannot smell cover me

Forgotten shadows find me

Guardians of the moon, please protect me
Nymphs of the still pools, please protect me
Skywatchers of heaven's fire, please protect me
Towering spirits of the date palm oasis, please protect me

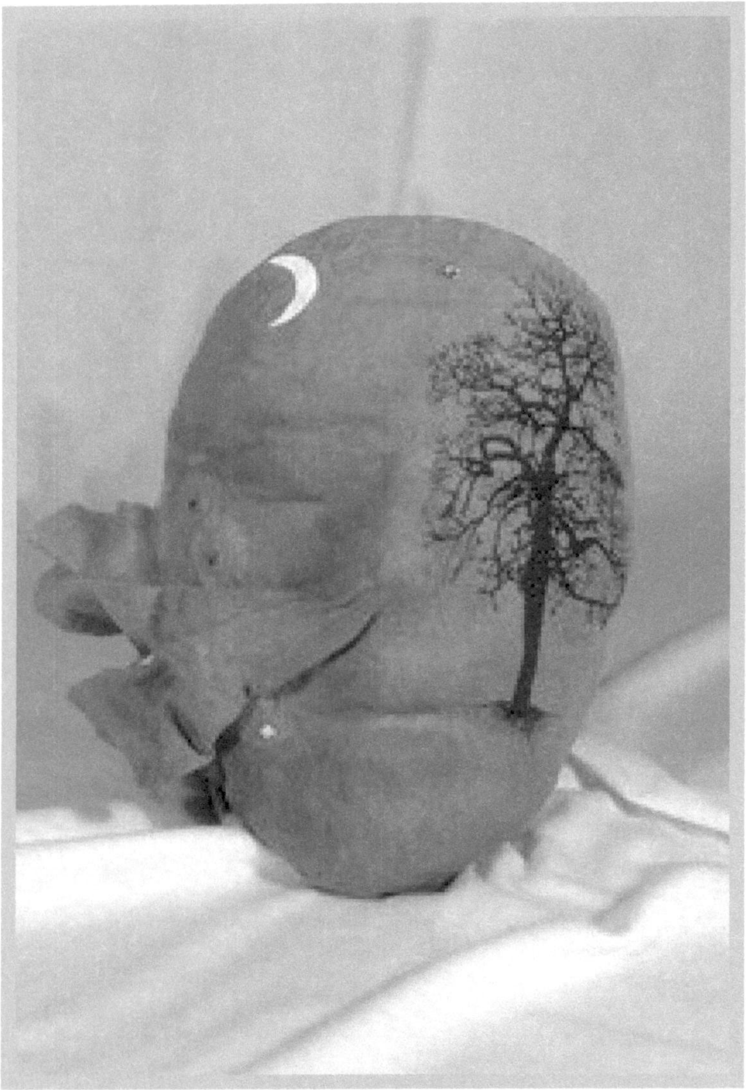

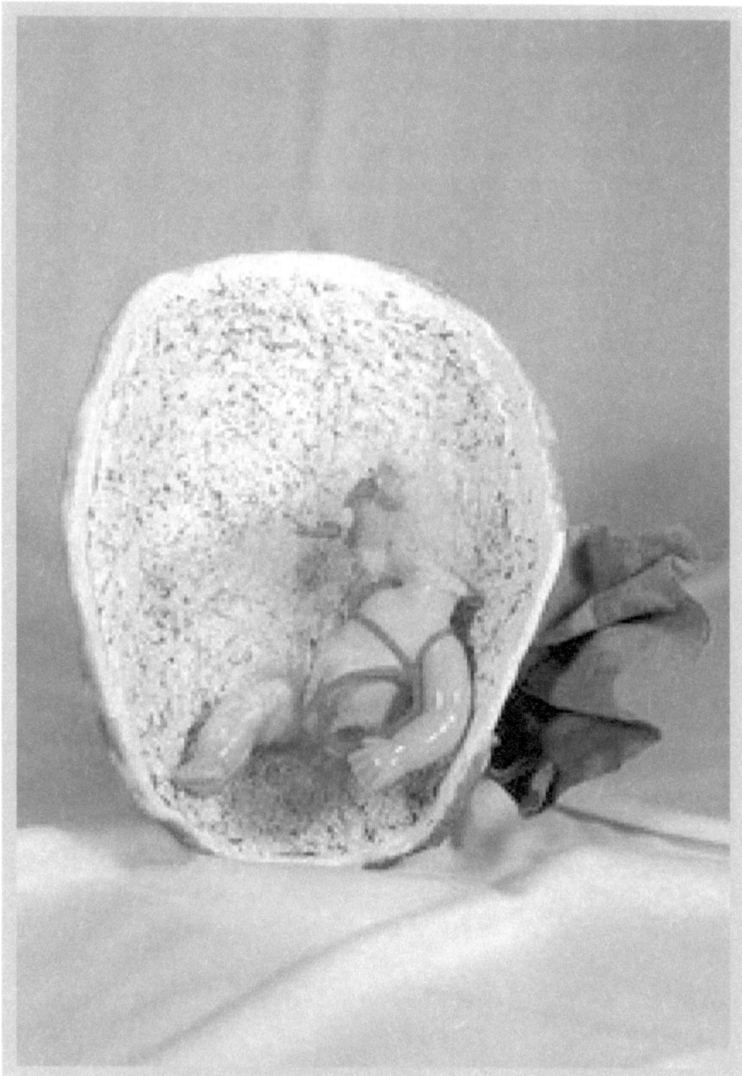

El umbral del bosque

In this darkest of woods there is, I hear,
A shadow tree. Once it was a living tree filled with bird's nests
And papery wings of masquerading butterflies.
Standing on the edge of tree-filled darkness, I taste my terror.
No lighted paths lead through.

In this darkest of woods there is, I hear,
A shadow tree. Once it was a living tree filled with bird's nests
And motionless, resting butterflies. Clothing the tree with wings
As still as fluttering leaves, these silent monarchs of the forest
Waited for winter's sun to heat their wings into spirals of golden prayer.

Intruding into chaotic tangles of bleak, dead stillness,
I notice the absence of butterflies.
Alone, now, so very alone in this thick quiet, I sought the shadow tree
But have stumbled, instead, into Ereshkigal's enchanted forest.

In this darkest of woods there is, I hear,
A shadow tree. Once, centuries ago,
It was a living tree filled with bird's nests
And sweet living butterflies poised for flight.
In search of the shadow tree, I stumbled into this dank grove.
Intoxicated with the pain and grief of years
I clutch life to me.
Knowing not the mysteries of Ereshkigal's gateways
I prostrate myself on the forest floor.
Silent and afraid, I wait for the shadow tree to find me.

In this darkest of woods there is, I hear,
A shadow tree. Surrounded by living trees

It stands unmarked and unnoticed.
Now only unspoken echoes
On the forest's floor speak of its ghostly presence.
Butterflies and birds are all gone. No papery rustle or
warning call
Mark the place of the tree.

Shrill rumors of shadow trees
Are whispered to be cross-stitched
On the borders of the altar cloth on Ereshkigal's high table.

El santo lugar

Mired in silence
In this darkest of woods where there is, I hear,
A shadow tree, I wait.
In the menacing darkness, I search my bags for a proper
offering.

Leaving behind that which I cannot carry with me,
I carry bundles of gifts to Ereshkigal's altar.
The delicious apple with living seeds;
A draught of crushed, fermented grapes;
Unseeing eyes: each of these and more I carefully place.

Weeping and shuddering, I collapse.

THE SEVEN GATES

HEARING VOICES FROM BELOW

LA ENTRADA PRIMERA / THE FIRST GATE

Morning star, direct my waking
Evening star, guide my dreaming
Help me find my way home
Help me. Help me.
Help me.
Help!

Un dolor fuerte

Walking this path among golden flowers and lacy ferns
I find no pleasure in its beauty.
Only faint memories of giggling under night's covers remain
When the moon was full and the night star radiant.

Once, twice, a multitude of times
I have murdered all my dreams and fed them to the ghostdogs
Who walk here with me.
But, in the moment of their killing
I forgot to post a guard at their grave
So they could not return to haunt me.
Now, I walk their receiving line
To shake each hand
To kiss each cheek.

Los días de los muertos

I count my dead
Like beads on a rosary.
I count my dead
Like inches on a yardstick.
I count my dead
Like pennies in a pig.
I count my dead
Like a flagellant's knots.
I count my dead
Like steps in a slow dance.

Derramamiento de sangre

My body bleeds its distrust of this path
While I dally on its perimeters examining bugs and beetles.

Los terremotos grandes

I have crossed through a gate I did not see.
I have passed under a portal I did not know existed.

Innocence has been mauled
Simplicity has been assaulted

Contentment has been attacked
Vulnerability has been abused

There are secret corridors here
There are chaotic labyrinths here

Harmony has been corroded
Trust has been disrupted
Joy has been buried alive
Abundance has been plundered

I have passed through a doorway I did not recognize
I have passed over a threshold I did not perceive.

THE SHATTERED FACE

LA ENTRADA SEGUNDO / THE SECOND GATE

Where the eye goes not
Where the ear goes not
Where the tongue goes not

I search for the stillness

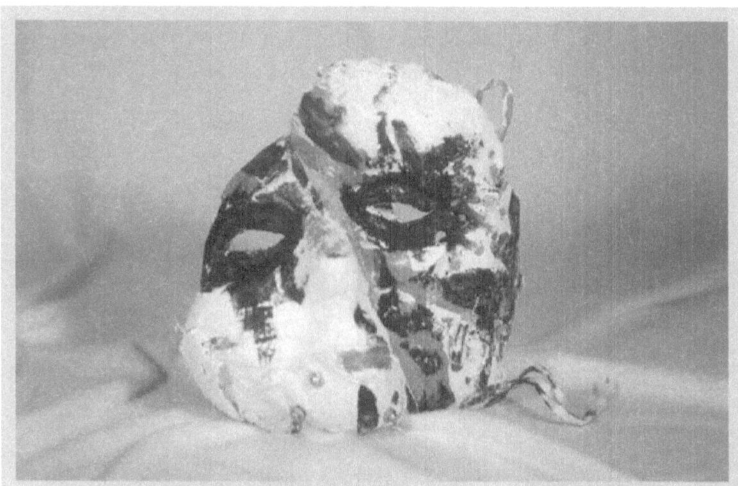

La neblina

Last night owl stalked me
Calling out the corners of her kingdom.
Her wings covered earth's shadows with their own.
Under this dying moon, she came near
And I knew her.

Bajo la lluvia

Was it just yesterday
I sat securely in the chair he'd carved for me from my
living tree
Whose roots and branches had once held heaven and earth
together?
When the raging river ripped away its capturing bank of
ochre clay;
When the huluppu tree tumbled sideways into the cairn of
river rubble;
When the roots let go of their mothering soil:
I reached into threatening waters to rescue the tree from its
destiny
And prayed we would not, together, be swept away by watery
angers.

Was it just yesterday
I sat at ease in the chair he'd carved for me from my
living tree
Whose roots and branches had once held heaven and earth
together?

El viento cortante

He seeded my world and in the loving of him
I was made complete.
In seeing myself reflected in his eyes
I opened from within and without.

He took the tree I'd rescued from the raging waters
And planted it in my garden where it grew tall and free.
Each morning the tree covered us with its green shadows.

Each evening birds sang a night song as a ripening moon hid in its branches.

Hearing other calls from the wild world within his spirit
He walked away from my garden.
Just before leaving me behind
He carved this chair which I sat in yesterday.

Los sueños de la noche

Last night under owl's shadow
I dreamed again of him.
Staring out over memories of a thousand mustard-gold rivers
It was his face I saw reflected in the hidden scrying waters.

The dream brought him as close as a shared whisper
Under thick down coverlets.
Banished and denied longings
Drew him as close as the bed clothing which covered me.

Completing the carving, he'd walked away without looking back.
Watching him leave, I locked the garden gate behind him.
I moved into outbuildings with small lanterns to light the night
And coarsely ground porridge to begin each day.

He left and the chair, carved from the tree he'd planted in my garden,
Became the seat of misery and grief. I covered it with muslin.
I carried the chair, carved from my powers,
And shrouded it away where I could not see it.

Nevertheless, in last night's dreams
He slipped, unbidden, back into my bed.
In feeling him enter, I was opened once more from within and without.
We looked deep into each other's kohl-lined eyes.

Ruinas de las nieblas

Yesterday, I pulled yards of coarse muslin
From my chair and carried it into the sun.
I sat in this chair which his hands had so deliberately carved
From my heart's living tree.
I pondered why he thought I needed such a chair
When I could lie on grass-covered earth and sing to the
songbirds;
When I could fly upwards towards the sun to soar in circles
with the hawks.

Asking the gods to return my inner living tree to me
I pulled the chair into the sun's warmth.
Asking the gods to return my inner powers
I cursed again his cutting down the living tree of my garden.

Yesterday I un-shrouded the elaborately carved chair
And tugged it into day's brightest light.
I sat in this chiseled chair
He'd so precisely created from my living tree.
I pondered why, before leaving me,
He had insisted upon carving such a chair
When I could sip honeysuckle nectar with the moths;
When I could whirl like a dust devil in silver light
And feel Owl's shadow cover me.

La ventana abierta

Last night after he left me to sleep alone once more
I heard repeating voices call me
From dark underplaces of knowing.
I heard them speak my most hidden names
From unknown depths below the cloud shadows of dawn.
Hearing them begin again, I wrapped myself inside yards of
white mist
But worried over their persistent callings.

La estrella más brillante de la mañana

Getting up with the morning star
I left the silent sleeping room
Where so embraced in sleep
He'd entered me once more

I faced east, said my morning prayers
And asked the skygods to protect my day.

I poured liquid incense into the censer
And lit it with a tiny ember from last night's blazing bonfire.

I raised a chalice of fermented fig wine
And poured it onto the ground with dawn's first sunrays.

I baked a fresh loaf of bread
And split its steam wide open with my bare hands.

Getting up with the morning star
I left my sleeping room
And begged the gods to tell me
Why he'd returned once more.

Ritos de purificación

Outside the clouds empty their stored jar of waters;
Inside I search my cupboards for the lost gate key.
Outside the winds torment dead leaves into a frenzy
Inside I empty my life's closet shelves.

El portón del jardín

I stand on one side of the gate
Staring at the mud-filled path that calls.
Overhead, clouds hide the morning sun;
Inside my garden, the birds stay silent.

I know I must walk through this carved gate
Leaving behind what must be left
But first I must mourn the destruction of my living tree.

I kindle a blazing fire and burn this chair he'd so carefully
carved.

On the gate's other side I post the hobo's mark
To warn the world of wanderers
About a vacated garden
Where a shrouded chair had been burned and its ashes
scattered.

I gather my cloak around head and shoulders.
I lift my bags. As I turn the rusted lock
A cloudburst empties the skies.
I walk on through.

SPLIT APART AND SEPARATED

LA ENTRADA TERCERA / THE THIRD GATE

Light of the night sky, walk with me in beauty
Light of the day sky, walk with me in illumination
Light of the inward sky, walk with me in joy

I do not know this path
I do not recognize its crossroads
I do not see its guardian tree
I cannot foretell where it leads

Light of the night sky, walk with me in beauty
Light of the day sky, walk with me in illumination
Light of the inward sky, walk with me in joy

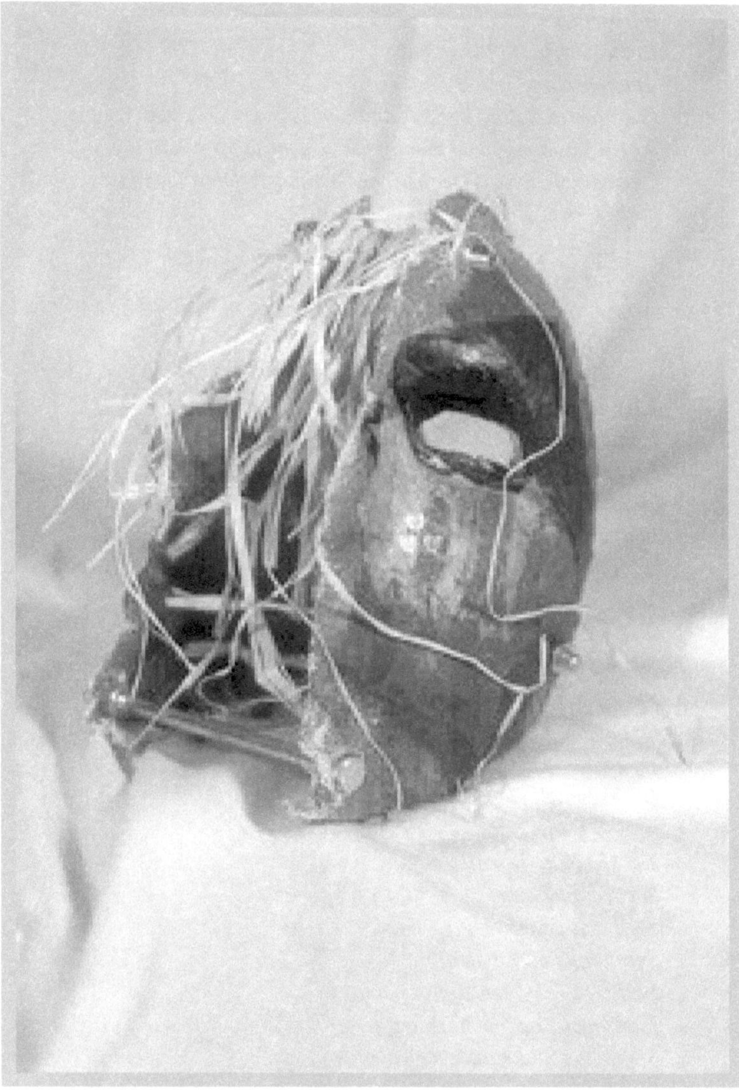

El portón

I place my ear to the ground
And when it is securely settled
Hear hisses, belches, grunts and moans.
These noises originate from hidden places so far below
I wonder if they rise to meet me, knowing before I know it,
That I must journey to their source.

I marvel at these most unseemly noises
Ascending from earth's depths like clouds of mosquitoes at
twilight.

Las aguas amargas

Picking up a discarded water skin
I fill it from the dying edge of summer's rain pool.

Stuffed into my tattered and stained ancestral carpet bag
This hoarded water
Must sustain me now as I touch my bared feet
To the dirt of narrow, rocky paths.

Slowly picking my way among boulders
Once more I wonder at the hissing voices:
Insistently they call me by my most intimate names
But never tell me how they know them.

La lluvia desnuda

South-rising rains
Spill water upon water,
Pour water over water,
Fold water into water,
Layer water on top of water,
Slip water underneath water,
Meld water into water.

Battering winds
Beat all waters into frenzied rivers
That flood earth's alluvial plain.

Growing steeper and darker as these scolding rains
Lash the earth, finally the path itself becomes a river.
It has no mercy for solitary walkers
Who seek to reach places beyond this place.

El vendaval del sur
Screaming winds
Rip my garments into fraying ribbons.
Slashing waters seek out my nakedness
To attack it.

Raíces de los sueños oscuros
Inside this torrent of strafing winds and floods
Skin is no protection.
Stained wetness is everywhere.
No barrier holds against the raging storm;
No dam is secure; no reinforced gate holds.

Rising waters cover earth
Restlessly seeking distant seas.

Lágrimas y chillidos
Whipping winds
Smash against my face
With such passionate forcefulness
That I spin backwards.
With bare hands, I stop my fall.

I know these vicious winds with that private intimacy
Known only to pilgrims
Whose desperate search for shelter
In the middle of the night
Brings them hesitantly to unknown beds,
Brings them begging to unknown tables.

Los estrechos del cañón

I began this journey under dawn's shadow
When first I heard luring voices from below.
They insisted my journey was essential
If I were to see all there was to see,
To claim all there was to claim.

I noted the darkening skies – filled with menacing clouds –
And hesitated.

In marking my confusion about journeying -
My hesitation - the voices drummed themselves more loudly.
They knew my names – every name I'd ever called myself,
Every name given to me by others.

After wavering the morning away in fear,
I lifted my tapestry-covered carpetbag.
It was filled with almonds, dates, raisins and sweet chocolate
candies.
Like a schoolgirl on her way to exams,
I picked up my skin of waters
Before beginning my worried climb.

I slipped through the trailhead and walked among veined,
scarred boulders
Formed of tar and silt.
Rounding the first corner, I found myself on an unsecured
walkway
Constructed of river gravel and summer's decaying leaves.

I noted the purple skies – filled with lightning and thunder
And plunged into the canyon below.

I began this journey just this morning under dawn's shadow
When first I heard the commanding voices from below.
They insisted my journey was essential
If I were to see all there was to see,
To claim all there was to claim.

Una cascada grande

To get to this spot
I walked into uncertain canyons
And rock crevices so narrow
I knew I could not find my way back
The way I came.

To get to this point
I walked across dunes so high and windswept
I thought I might drown,
Unseen and un-mourned,
Under barren, shifting rivers of sand.

To get to this place
I slid down mountainsides so ragged
I thought I might fall straight down
Into isolated and undisclosed ravines.
I could not think about them without trembling.

Un puente de los recuerdos

Coming to a gated bridge
Barred shut but straining at its hinges,
I pause and consider the shreds of clothing
That reveal more of my journey
Than they conceal.

I watch prowling, teeth-bared dogs
Patrol the other side.
Silently they snarl their night-anxieties
Into distant footings of this groaning bridge.

La represión del río desenfrenado

Guardians of the estuary's floodgate
Remain quiet inside their fortress.

I wonder why they never hear the voices of the wind;
Why they never reveal the beauty of the forest.

I wonder why they never spotlight the evergreen trees by the banks;
Why tree branches must remain invisible in the moon's hiding.

Guardians of the estuary's floodgate
Ignore red paint spirals on my body.

Las mareas más fuertes
What in my ancestral carpet bag
Has heard the voice of the wind
And felt the song of the rain?

What voices lured me into this journey
From which I can never return
Untouched and unchanged?

El lugar del nacimiento del alma
I am unrecognizable to myself
Standing here
In harsh winds and rain
With clothing that does not conceal,
Skin that does not protect.

La mesa del sacrificio
To pass across the river safely,
Posted signs tell all who read
They must carry gifts for the river gods.

But I have not been told who they are
Nor have I been given a map
To find my way to the sacred shrines
Where all song is hushed,
All dance stilled.

Standing here and facing into the south wind's foreboding
I remember Ereshkigal's altar in the forest.
Days ago, with such clarity,

I knew what was required of me.

I consecrated the sacraments:
My tears were the wine.
My screams were the bread.
My prayers were the vinegar laced with water.

Here, the posted markers say, it is necessary
To appease the gate's guardians
With course bread and thick brown ale.
It is necessary to throw decaying bones
Into the circle of snarling dogs
So they will lie down on command.
It is necessary to offer stories, songs, and prayers
To whatever gods may hide among the shadows.

But my mouth is stilled and my throat is choked.

La catarata
I am furious at this endless strafing of wind and water;
I am furious because the sacred shrine is shrouded within thick mists;
I am furious at the barking dogs for their ceaseless noise;
I am furious because my eyes cannot find the path through the forest;
I am furious at my torn clothing and near-nakedness;
I am furious because there are no reliable maps;
I am furious at my helpless crying;
I am furious because I must beg with hands stretched out.

No puede ser
I open my water-rotted bag
With its broken clasps. I rummage its interior.
My eyes and hands ransack its secret pockets
To find what hidden morsels remain intact.
If only I can find some releasing tidbit
From my life journey
Perhaps I may inspire mercy from the silent watchers.

Perhaps I may pacify their noisy dogs.

In all of my rummaging
I find only fragmented, shattered and broken words.
These will not do!

Something else is called for.
Something more is asked for.

Las tormentas llegan otra vez

Rising waters from below
Drink from torrential rains so thick
I cannot see my hand at arm's length.
In my fury and rage
I raise my obscene fist into the sky.
I curse my journey.

Portones filtrantes

I have no gift for the table
Untouched by inner fury
At being trapped alone and outside.
In seeking a way across the raging river;
In seeking a way to escape these drenching rains;
In seeking a way into gentle shelters with firelit hearths;
In seeking a way to cover my ragged nakedness with soft, dry fleece;
I merge with the wind and rain.
I slip through to the altar of the river's gods.

Mesa de la esperanza silenciosa

I offer the table's presiding priestess the strength of my love
Yet know not if it is sufficient; know not if it is desired.

I offer the table's presiding priestess the presence of my hope
But wait in subdued silence to learn her judgment of its worth.

I offer the table's presiding priestess the warmth of my
laughter
But wait in trembling apprehension as she examines it.

I offer the table's presiding priestess the power of my life
Yet know not if it is enough; know not if it is welcome.

Los obsequios
Before she says yes or no to my presence at her table
She caresses my fragile gifts as if soothing a restless child.

She turns them over and over in her bent, crooked, translucent
fingers
Yet says nothing.

What she thinks of me, if anything at all,
I cannot tell.

Her eyes are shielded away from mine while she examines
My fragile offerings
With gnarled, arthritic hands.

Her words are silent.
She speaks not what she knows.

El silencio espeso
My offered collection of treasures must be enough.
No other gifts have survived the rain and wind.
This assortment of my treasures is all that remains.
No other gifts have been held back to place on her table.

She motions me to kneel and wait in silence.
In my weariness and depletion,
I shiver because she does not speak.

Her blind silent fury is terrifying.

THE WATCHER

LA ENTRADA CUARTA / THE FOURTH GATE

Spirit of wind open paths before me
Spirit of flame light horizons within
Spirit of water bathe away all fear
Spirit of earth raise me over and over again

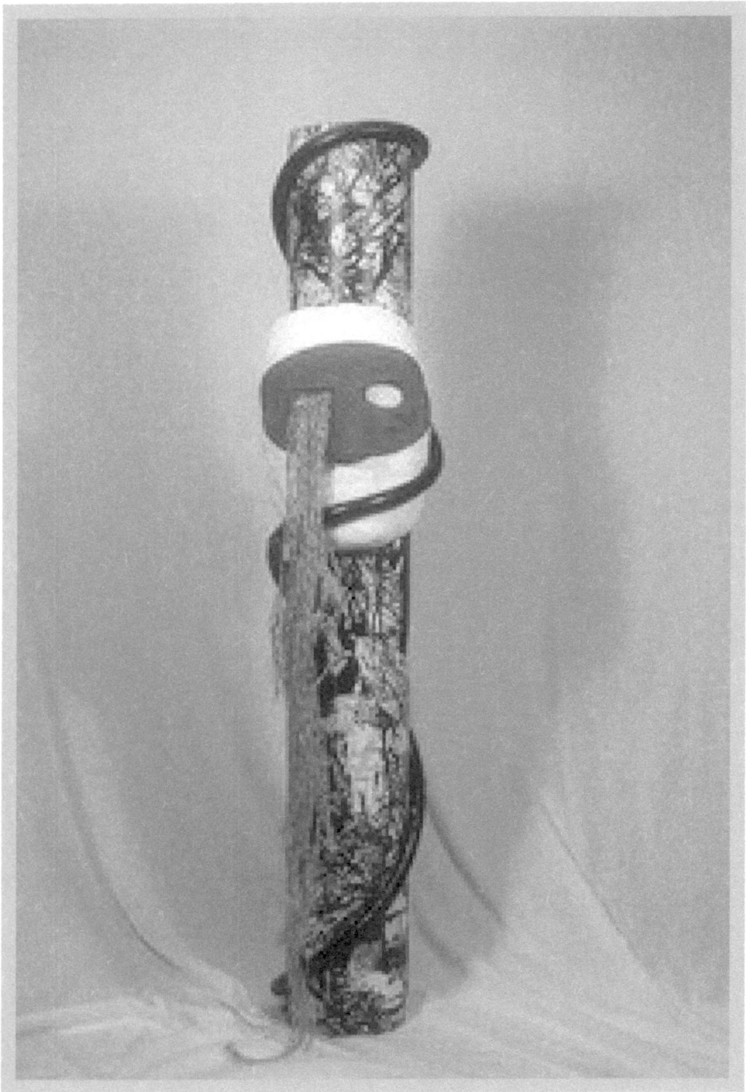

LA GARITA CERRADA

This bleak landscape
Whispers in my dreams.
It whispers in snags and tangles -
In brambles full of rotting berries.
Rumoring whispers tug at me
Like frozen thorns snatch bare skin
And rip it raw to bleeding.
All clothing is shredded into unbearable rags
And hung out for all passersby to see and pity.

Feeling the ground thunder below,
I rock all fears in shivering arms.
I try to quiet them
Yet they continue their loud squalling.

I am so alone here under this disapproving sky -
So alone and so isolated from yesterday's gods.
Already I am miles away from the gods' home
And the fortune-telling bones I threw there.
Yesterday I destroyed a thick welded gate
To continue this deliberate walking into desolation.
I travel but do not know my final destination.
Without guide or compass, I follow these nagging whispers
That only hint at the direction of my journey.

I scan distant mountain-filled horizons
For the brightly-shining evening star.
Ominous clouds hide her. I seek to find
Shelter from heaven's fire but find none.

My destination is a foreign land, one whose currency
I do not know; one whose language is incomprehensible
Without a dictionary which I do not have.
This land I slowly cross plays me no melody of bird or
human flute

There is an altar whose doorway I must enter,
Whose threshold I must pass.

I have not been told what incense to carry –
Whether copal or frankincense. I have no guarding servant.
I do not know what misshapen spirit will greet me.

I breathe in the terror of this tundra-night.
I spit out its clotted phlegm.

I search for a cool spring to rinse my throat of dust.
Instead, I find a bracken-filled well of bitter waters.

Barren vistas, each more austere than the last,
Greet each turn in the road.
Icy blasts fill the air with emptiness.
No coyote bays at my footsteps. No snake
Rustles its warning at my presence.
I turn a corner, climb a rock, stumble, fall, and cut my
hands.
Barring the path is a swinging gate. "State the
Destination of your journey," a hidden voice insists.
How do I tell this unseen gatekeeper that I do not know it?

I open my satchel and stir about inside it.
I hunt my passport with its photo of a tidy face and combed
hair.
In its place, however,
I find only a torn and vandalized booklet of outdated
stamps.

Here, at the entrance of a pass to a canyon I can see far
below,
I cannot continue. Soldiers of fortune,
With guns and frozen stares, stand guard here.
I must produce that which is demanded
Before I will be given my traveling papers with fresh stamps.

I cannot return the way I came. The only way forward is
through.
Stopped dead in my place by these guardians of the pass
I remove my terror that sparkles like just-polished crystal.
I offer it as a bribe. The gate swings open and I walk
through.

THE RED WHORE

LA ENTRADA QUINTA / THE FIFTH GATE

I light dawn's white candle,
Fill the empty silver chalice with mead,
Toss bread to the birds,
Empty the mind of all thoughts.

A new day has begun

El camino tortuoso

Last night while I watched the evening star climb steadily
Into moon's shadow, tall rumors hung among the trees.
Sleep, when it came, was restless.
Intrusive voices from below interrupted night's softness.

Caught again in strangling webs of fear
I heard my name. I felt dread dig deep into my belly.
My stuttering voice tried to answer but could not.
My heart clutched its fears and my soundless voice screamed.

Each night of this journey has brought old voices
To line out tuneless, irritating songs.
Inside my dream's landscapes, their obscene lyrics
Play hide and seek among my waking thoughts.

I tire of these songs but they round through me
Like monks' chanting fills the choir with holy prayers.
I weep at their torturing, off-key monotone.
I beg the voices to go away but they demand to be found.

Una esquina de la noche

Rising this morning before sun could force moon out of
her sky
I washed myself with water from an ice-skimmed bucket.
I boiled coffee with eggshells and drank the bitter brew
straight.
I chewed stale sourdough loaves like they were manna.

Dressing myself in layers of down and canvas
I plastered my face with astringent herbal potions.
Morning's chill touched inwards to rouse the bones
And eyes' longing watered the winds.

Los senderos despreciables

Leaving behind the shelter of night's dense oak forest,
I step over fallen trees

And lift strands of rusted barbed wire
To climb through forbidden fences.

Hand-printed signs on fire-blackened trees
Urge extreme caution.
They warn: the tiny spring is dry;
The water pump has no priming jar.

Following steep, narrow footpaths through posted fields
I watch last night's sacred datura blossoms close.
Wolf howls shatter the thick velvet silence.
Bleak shades laugh within it.

Alone on this faint trail, which sometimes is not a trail
at all,
My footsteps become an old woman's stumble.
From charcoaled trees, screeching black crows count my steps.
Overhead a vulture tribe hunts the dying for dinner.

Scanning earth's scat like priests read sacred texts,
I hope to find the gate of exits hidden somewhere
Among distant blood-red mesas. But this trail
Has seen no recent pilgrims and its scent is very old.

My decision to follow obnoxious voices has brought
me here
Far away from my sleepy oasis of date palms.
I lie down at night to dream and each morning I awaken
But I am not rested nor is my spirit quieted.

La plata de la marisma

As I walk, I feel more alone than I can bear.
Dread fills my body until my flesh feels as if it must break
in two.
Splitting me through my center and splaying this
Painful wound into the outer world.

My heart pounds and it is not from the walking.

Tenacious thoughts play a rhythm of drumbeats inside my skull.
I find no joy in the distant buttes that jut towards heaven,
No pleasure in the rain clouds which cool summer's heat.

When evening announces its arrival by
Lengthening lavender and gold shadows,
A cloud of bats covers moon's tiniest silver crescent;
A Great Horned Owl hoots at its mate.

In the distance a flickering orange and blue neon sign
Announces a house of the night
Where pilgrims purchase pleasure, or sleep, for a bronze coin.
I stand outside the doorway to beg a pitcher of cold beer.

The old whore who answers my pounding knock
Is cross-dressed and painted bright red.
She grabs my face and demands to know why I travel here.
With trembling voice I answer but she does not believe me.

I stand in the doorway, first on one foot and then the other.
I seek to appease her wrath but don't understand what she says.
I have no magic coin to sleep peacefully under her roof.
My confusion grows; I shatter the silence with begging.

She sends for the man behind the bar.
Rudely they discuss my request for beer, bread, and a bed.
They ask what I can pay.
They ask what offering I will make to the flickering candle shrine.

Lacking the coin of the house, I bend low to check my pack.
In ripping, raging greed, the she-bitch who rules this house
Steals my neck's lapis blue beads as the virginal offering.
With tiny, bony fingers she gifts them to the doorway's goddess.

Fearing what lies ahead, I cross the doorframe.
I paint myself blue and green with flowers everywhere.
I gulp newly brewed rough-edged ale from chipped pottery.
I have found the gate of exits and it has pulled me through.

THE GUARDIANS

LA ENTRADA SEXTA / THE SIXTH GATE

Soaring eagle who plays inside swift updrafts
Leaping dolphin who dives under crashing waves
Singing cicadas who slowly climb skyward
Burning cypress who smolders nearby

Carry my prayers
To whatever gods will listen

Memorias silenciadas

Lava bubbles erupt now with a pulse of their own.
Odors of death fill the unmoving air:
These are omens from earth's most hidden womb.
Seeking entry to the valley below, I dodge liquid fire.

Landscape smells are familiar with gases and melted rock
When I seek to know where I am
No recognizable traces of living history remain. The past
Is buried beneath charred leaves and tall ghost trees.

Objetos y artefactos espirituales

Others have forgotten this path and its gods are all in hiding.
Nevertheless, voices belch and beckon from molten fissures below.
Vile petroglyphs sketch forgotten directions. Other solitary pilgrims
Carved their memories in hardened volcanic ash.

Stone piles mark the prayers of the dead and carved gates report
Remembered handprints of blood.
Custodians, older than the stone piles,
Question each isolated seeker who wanders here. In this
deserted land even the dust is examined for signs.

Documentos de identidad

Breath comes in gasps. Fear and stench steal it
Away from my clenched, determined mouth.
Overhead, raven paces its flight by my faltering steps.
I look for a sweet spring of water, an oasis in this never-ending desert,
But find only boiling sulfuric pools surrounded by salt.

I forget why I began this journey. I can't imagine why I wanted
To enter the world below -
That world whose palatial cave I know only by rumors.

What was I thinking when I packed my bags? All that remains
Is a tiny waist pack filled with paper mementos of a past that is no more.

Paredes de barrao y portales de hiero

The descent is slow
Each step is just a stone away from a broken body –
From a body that is unable to rise again.
The horizon is hidden:
The path covered with long shadows.
In the distance I see palm trees
And a huge pool of turquoise water.

With outstretched arms, I begin to run.

The mirage fills my nose with the scent of hibiscus and flowering plumeria.
It comforts my feet.
It soothes my wind-scarred eyes.
It bathes my skin in rapture.
I rush forward to swim in its waters.

Entrance, however, is denied.
Posted guardians of the gate deny me access.

Por vía de los sueños

In this boundary between erupting volcanoes
And inner visions of unrippled lake mirrors
I lie down to rest. Overhead, ospreys ride unseen winds
To find stillpoints for their wings. Here on the boundary
Between the worlds, I know I must go forward.
I must recall how to satisfy these custodians
Of the portal to the world below.

In the pause between breaths: In the moment of lying down,
An image fills the eyes and occupies the ears.

Music drums a heartbeat cadence. The frightened mind slows.
Suddenly I remember: this is an altar; a threshold; a doorframe.
Proper offerings must be placed.

Wounded and weakened by my desperate journey,
I find only old papers in my threadbare waist pack.

Ojo de Agua

These mute gate watchers have no use for hoarded identity papers
They do not care to collect old memories like stone piles at the gate
They have no way to transform a traveler's wounds
They know no way to heal questioning pain

They watch in silence as I unbuckle the pack wrapped 'round my belly.
Slowly I open it and wonder what gift remains.
Dumping papers and memories on the ground,
I sift through them with scratching fingers.

These treasures I brought with me have no value here.
They must, the watchers make clear, be left behind.
Enraged at these guardians of the gate and their prohibitions,
I find a fear so primitive, it has no name.

Un sacrificio para los jueces

Watching me scream icy fear and blazing rage
Judges of this gate's pilgrims stare steadily into nothingness.
They whisper what I already know.
From this moment forward, there is no regress.
You must find the proper offering and it must be given.
My protests echo in a storm of shouts and tears.
Nevertheless, the barrier is clear.
There is no way through without a sacrificial gift.

Still wishing it could be otherwise, I slowly unpeel my skin.
Like a snake, I writhe and wriggle and some inner rind of transparency
Glows like a beckoning sun. While the motionless censors watch,
An inner gate shifts and opens.

Leaving behind all that was before, I walk through.

PICASSO FACE

LA ENTRADA SEPTIMA / THE SEVENTH GATE

Earth be my ground:
May you gentle my steps.

Air be my breath:
May you empty me of terror.

Fire be my shield:
May you fill me with warmth.

Water be my healing:
May your artesian wells purify my rage.

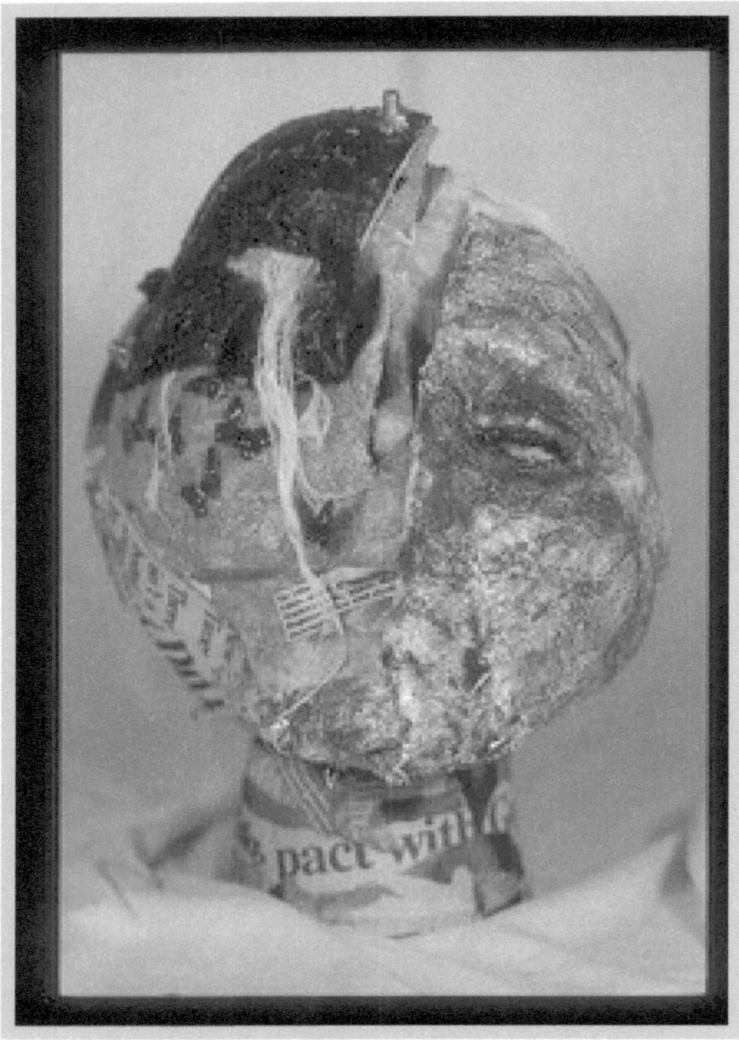
pact

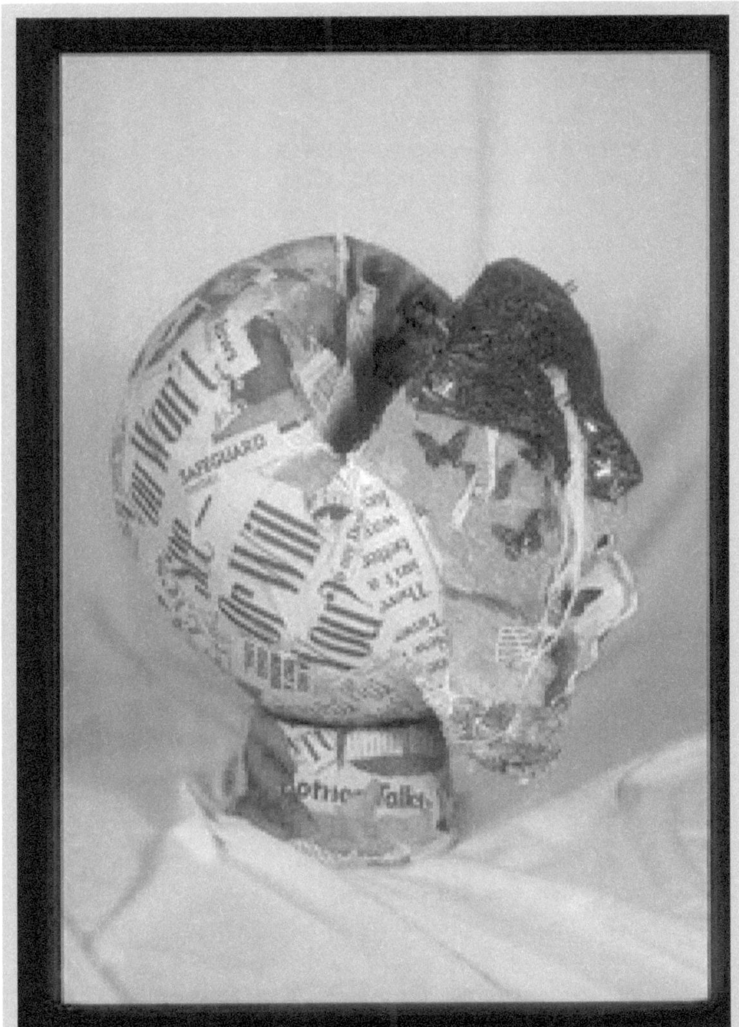

El silencio gris y deprimente

Swirling dense fog causes my feet to waver.
I cannot remember the sun.
For months I have wandered here:
Creating a path between granite boulders;
Descending into mist-enshrouded valleys.
Sounding the closeness of deep, wide, and impenetrable rivers
Has brought me here.
I circle falling waters without sight.

Bajo la sombra del sol

Down the center of this split forest,
Boiling whitewater rapids
Steal whatever they can to carry it away.

My body feels unbalanced on clay paths.
Hand follows hand as I search the ground
For new inches of safety.

There is no path from here to
River estuaries that spill topsoil into swelling waves
Of unnamed oceans.

The passageway to the west is lost.
There is no path from here
To there.

Las cataratas del terror

Assaulted each day by blowing mists
I wonder if ever again
I can find my way into open fields at dawn,
Smell wild iris in high mountain meadows.
Hear hummingbirds buzz trumpet vines for nectar,
Watch twilight's deer feeding at the forest's edge,
Feel the music of the aurora borealis in my pulse,
Taste iced champagne under the solstice full moon,
Touch the morning star with my heart,

Sense the sweet catch of breath when skies open after a
storm,
Emerge intact from this dark night.

Cerro de la serpiente

At the edge of torrential rivers
I know, but cannot see, the power of tumbling waters.
My bare feet feel the thundering call to come closer.

I walk blind in mid-day's darkness.
It is always night here.
There is no trace, within or without, of the solar star.

I walk alone in this forest of shadow trees,
Under carpets of air born moss.
Thick webs grab my face.

Plunging waterfalls
Thunder their god's name
In all of earth's common tongues.

In all my walking dreams,
Pervasive, hushed voices name this time and this place
As all there is.

Breathing thick vapors, I hold my ears against the roaring.
I cannot retrace my steps.
Last night's path is already washed away and lost.

I know the raging voice of this river
Like a mariner recognizes the surge of waves
Just before heavy seas quiet.

El jardin del sol caliente

Many lifetimes ago I stood alone
In a sunny garden
With my transplanted huluppu tree.

Years before I'd rescued it
From raging waters.
Its clinging rootlets
Once sunk deep into baked blood-red clays
Had been washed bare by pounding bitter rains.
Kaleidoscopic breezes darted here
And skipped there.
Soft winds refracted mid-day's common colors
Into a rainbow of shattering prisms
That swept the morning clean.

The eclipsing sun caressed my face
With a soft gentleness so tender
For hours I wept under my tree.
Overhead the leaves rustled with forgotten memories:
Within its leafy shadows, a thousand sun-moons danced on the grass.

Many lifetimes ago I stood alone
In my garden
With the transplanted huluppu tree.

Years before I'd rescued it
From storm-filled riverbanks.
I sang it a song of storms and ochre red rivers.
The tree sang its own remembered tales as well
And gentled my griefs with sturdy tenderness.

La cueva sin salida

In my childhood I heard whispered tales about an enchanted cave
With magical passageways and gates hidden by dense fogs.
I heard songs about shadow forests
So protected by thorn bushes no one could enter.
Or, more precisely spoken, they said:
No one could enter and return home again.

Singing voices of traveling story-tellers

Hinted at hidden subterranean rooms filled with healing crystals
And obscured veins of smoked gold.
They spoke of caverns that must be entered
In the dark between the old and new moons,
And through stone-hidden gates.
Paths, they said, into these caverns led to cleansing pools
Where a traveler's mud-crusted weariness could yield to sleep.

Storytellers who themselves had never visited the world below
Gossiped that eternity's candles sooted the walls black.
Thick spicy incense perfumed the air.
In the outer passageways, they reported, it was possible to get lost
And wander for years.
But, they insisted, having entered the underground cave
Of darkness and silence
Each pilgrim eventually came upon the last gate.

Entering the gate, they claimed, required that a song or a story
Be offered to the watchers of the gate. The legend of the gate
Spoken in guarded whispers by those who had never seen it,
Foretold that the gate never swung open until the seeker
Told her story in words that stripped her secrets bare
And offered up all smuggled treasures.

Once having found the mist-covered entrance of the gate,
The traveler must kneel and crawl on hands and knees
Into earth's most hidden healing cave.

The seeker must call out, in a clear voice, her reasons for seeking to enter.
Here, at this moment, other voices will join her own,
Other stories will seek her out.

Not knowing why, the storytellers say,

Each seeker of the world below dies.

Los rapidos del dolor

Lost in a forest where every tree is a shadow:
Alone with a grove of shadow trees whose roots dig deep into
earth's belly:
I make a bed and lie down to sleep.

In my dreams, I sing more sorrowfully than the doves
And the gate's watcher weeps.
Slowly, as if rusted shut for centuries, the door swings open.

Totally alone among the shades,
I grasp the gate's posts with my hands.
Naked, I kneel between their void.

Separated from everything I know
I bow low to enter the dust-filled world
That calls me by my true names.

ERESHKIGAL

UNA MUJER MORIBUNDA / A DYING WOMAN

Walk with me
Watch over me
Stand outside the gate I have entered
Remember me and do not forget

Ring bells
Sing songs
All creation demands dying
So that earth may be reborn.

Remember me and do not forget
Stand outside the threshold I have crossed
Watch over me
Wait with me

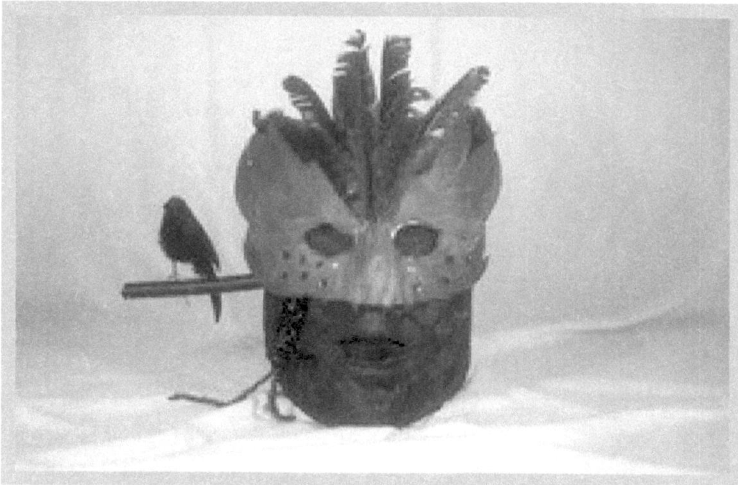

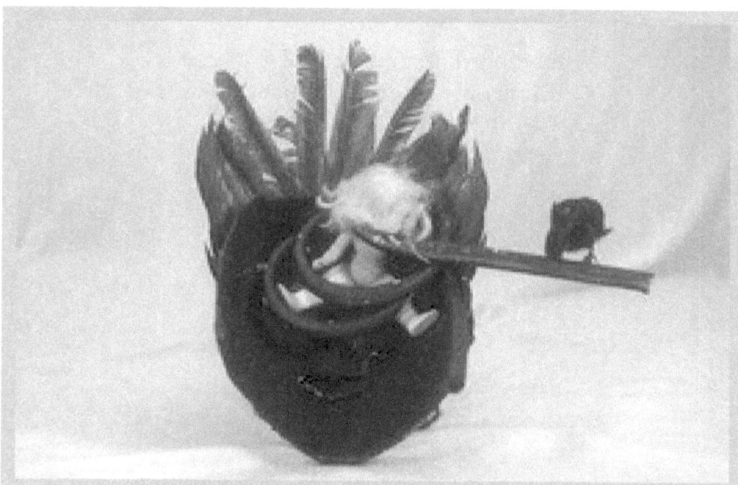

El tiempo del nacimiento del alma

It is so silent here.
Dust covers everything:
Even the food offered to the gods
Is filled with dust.

Unseen and unheard
I wait in the dark silence of nights
When there is no moon.
Untouched and uncomforted
I hang suspended in the emptiness of brooding
Where there is no illumination.

It is so silent here.
Dust covers everything:
Even my body offered to the gods of this cave
Is filled with dust.

Las ofrendas del mundo

It is said that suffering makes us wise
And becomes our truest teacher.

It is said that suffering is a result of sin
And by repenting we can stop its ravaging of our spirits.

It is said that suffering is due to our attachments
And all we need to do is to let them go.

It is said that suffering is inevitable
And by accepting our fate we can live honorably.

It is said that suffering is karmic
And by this life we redeem our past.

It is said that suffering is what makes us most human
And that we can offer it our thanks.

It is said that suffering is caused by our weakness

And by choosing to be strong we can grow beyond it.

It is said that suffering is our rite of purification for rebirth
And by embracing it we are transformed.

It is said that suffering connects us most deeply with others
And by drinking from the well of suffering we learn, at last,
compassion.

Reflexiones del mundo de los árboles de las sombras

Naked and suffering
I hang between the worlds
And hope life is stronger than death.

OWL'S SHADOW

LA CUEVA / THE CAVE

Seven gates I have walked through.
Seven guardians I have met.
Seven offerings I have left behind me.
Seven altars have received my prayers.

Nothing remains but dust-covered silence

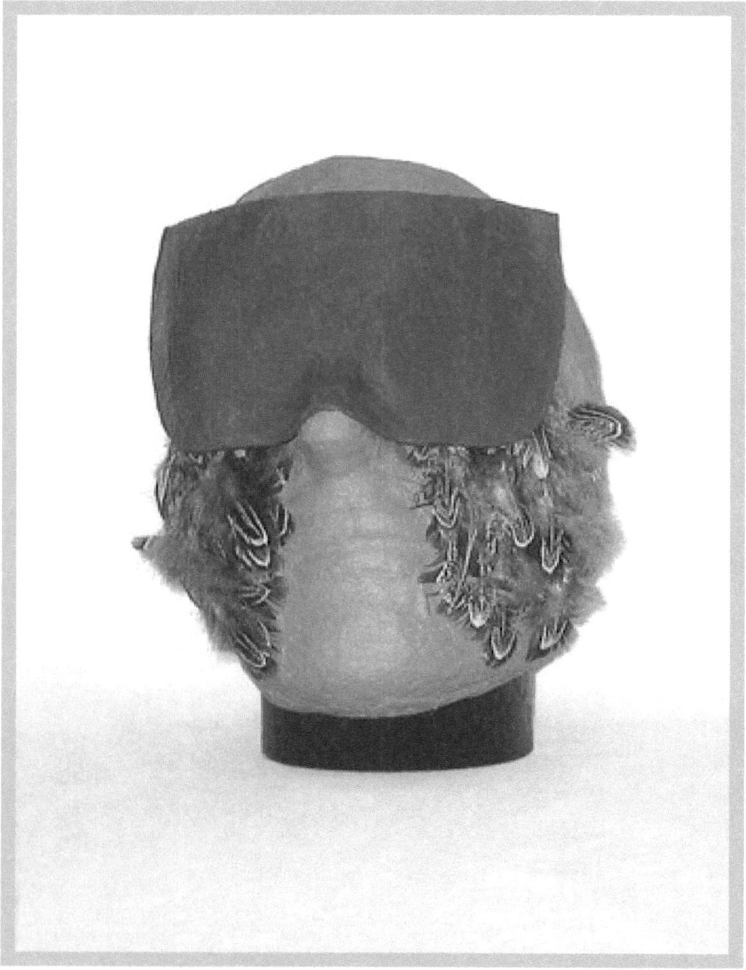

Mi hermana y mi enemiga

Beloved Sister:
Hearing the voices of centuries
In moon's darkness
My name is courage.
Listen to my heart's song
For I have never forgotten you.

Sky's wind
Heaven's Fire
Scarlet roses wrapped in fragrant myrtle leaves
Ocean's summer fogbanks:
All these, and more, I carry for you.

Where is your house which you never leave?
Where is the road which you never travel?
Where is the lintel under which you never pass?
Where is the window which you never throw open?

Richly seeded pomegranates
Caged white doves
Water lilies and sea anemones
Censers smoking with myrrh:
All these, and more, I carry for you

Listen to my heart's song
For I have never forgotten you.

Hated Sister:
Hearing the voices of centuries
In moon's darkness,
My name is fear.

Alone and bleeding
I struggle between the worlds
And wait for the waters that contain death.

Isolated and weeping

I search between the worlds
And discover the soul's labyrinth understands death.

Abandoned and despairing
I dance between the worlds
And trust the heartbeat's rhythms to transform death.

Silent and speechless
I hear the music between the worlds
And begin to sing my resurrection.

INTERLUDE

CHAOS CREATES TRANSFORMATION

UNA MUJER QUE NACE / BIRTHING WOMAN

May she be trusting and cautious
May she be strong and gentle
May she be reasonable and emotional
May she be prudent and properly disrespectful
May she be laughing and crying
May she be full of simplicity and limitless complexity
May she be innocent and knowing
May she be completely and joyously begotten

May the winds of heaven be gracious to her
May the waves of the sea support her
May the flowers of earth teach her
May thunder and lightning protect her

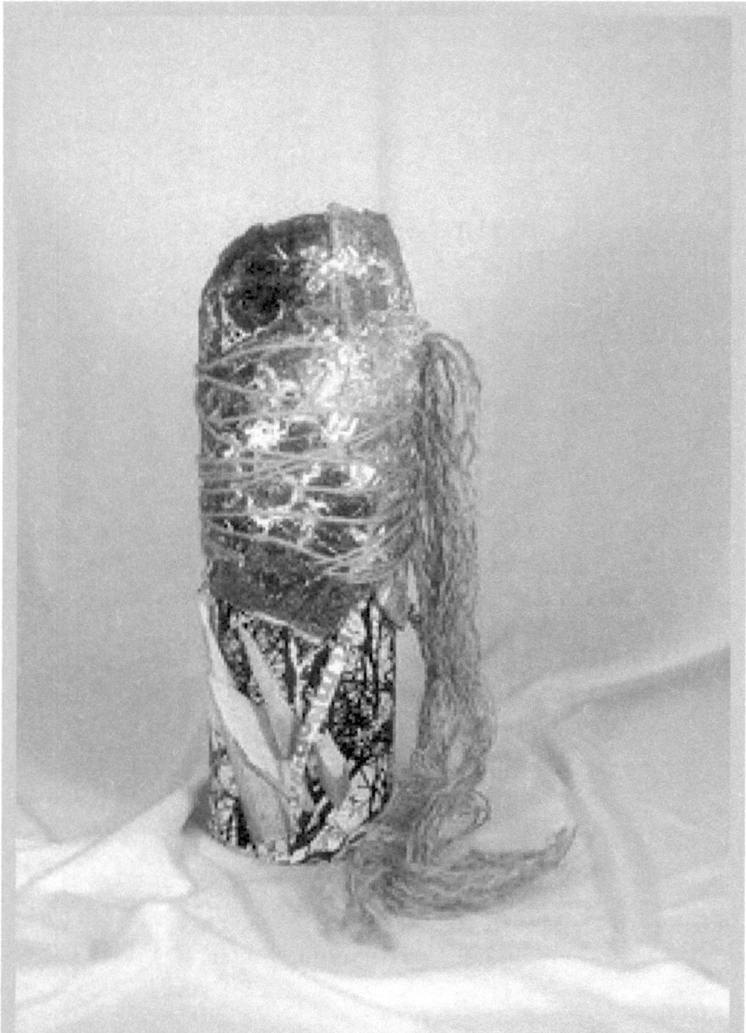

La matriz del tiempo consciente

A woman who decides, however she decides,
To give birth to a new self
Nevertheless shrieks loud grief for her old dead self
But silently *so no one may hear her.*

Even though her mind knows beforehand
That in these matters death always precedes new life
The day of her dying is filled with surprise.
She mourns, alone and unattended,
For that which she must give up, shed, and toss away.

The loss of easy habits and conventional gestures;
The absence of midwives boiling water;
A deep inner ambivalence about such a pregnancy:
All of these, and more, snake-like
Create a shedding of identity.
A familiar, beloved and comfortable skin must be left
behind.

Insistent upon birthing a new self
She first clutches and then reluctantly discards
All her costly embroidered shrouds of pain.

For courage, she reminds herself constantly
About deliberate and bloody altars
Where she repeatedly bargained away her old self.

The woman who decides, however she decides,
To conceive a new self
Blushes with sudden speechless shyness at her temerity,
Weeps with awareness of her bravery.

Like distant gods, however it is that she makes such
decisions,
She simply decides
That she will create something new:
She decides it is now time to give birth to herSelf.

The woman who decides,
However it is that she decides such matters,
To conceive and give birth to a new self,
This woman rushes inward
To congratulate herself on her wisdom.
She shouts with freedom at her liberation.
A woman who decides,
However a woman makes such a decision,
To give birth to herSelf,
Rejoices that she has thought of such a thing at all.
She stands under the new moon,
Flexing and rippling her birth muscles.
She stretches like a Persian cat just awake from sleeping.
And, afterwards,
She flings her body upside down and somersaults joy.

In the full moon's voluptuous light she skips a path into being
Between cosmos, rosemary, and fragrant lavender.

Catching fireflies,
Tugging at spider webs,
Teasing a ground beetle,
She whistles with a blade of grass between her teeth.

Coming to a moment just before the moment of her birthing
She squats in the time of the dark moon
And ponders what she has done.
In that fertile darkness of brooding silence and waiting
She enters the night sky to divine the signs.
With awe and reverence she weaves herSelf
A bright red ribbon to wear around her left wrist.
She crochets an indigo silk sleeping cap
To protect her from hostile winds and
Embroiders a cashmere dreaming blanket to shelter her fears,
To comfort her times of aloneness.

El momento en que se va la coronilla
She sees, hears, and feels again.

She is fully alive and working with all her powers.

She is grunting and farting.
She is bleeding and open.
She is pushing and resting.
Pushing and resting,
Resting and pushing.
She is resting and pushing.
She is open and bleeding.
She is farting and grunting.

She is softly whimpering.
She is loudly screaming at the top of her lungs.
She is sobbing and singing and laughing.

It is now her time and she is claiming it as her own.

Dar a luz
She has risked creation
She has become a she-goddess pregnant with a new universe
She is going to give birth to herSelf.
Her labor has just begun.

HOMELAND

INANNA, QUEEN OF HEAVEN

CRUZANDO LA FRONTERA / CROSSING THE BORDER

Come close:
Let your waters heal me.
Sing to me and I will sing back to you

Embrace me in your love.
Help me surrender to life's beauty.

Come closer:
Let your waters heal me.
Sing to me and I will sing back to you.

Carry me skywards while I reach towards the sun.
Help me surrender to life's dance.

Come closer still:
Let your waters heal me.
Sing to me and I will sing back to you.

Una canción para el cielo

On this day my breath is strong and pure:
I breathe and know I am breathing.

On this day my ears are attentive:
I listen and know I am hearing.

On this day my eyes are open:
I watch and know I am seeing.

On this day my pace is measured and steady:
I walk and know I am walking.

Una canción para los océanos

On this day my heart is at ease:
I open it and know it is opening.

On this day my mind is peaceful:
I still it and know it is quiet.

On this day my spirit is free:
I unfetter it and know it is celebrating.

On this day my body is awake:
I touch it and know that it knows me.

Una canción para el bosque

On this day my voice is playful:
I tease the gods and hear their ripples of laughter.

On this day my hands are graced:
I play the flute and hear its sweet cadences.

On this day my legs are strong:
I climb steadily and recognize the path.

On this day my life is content:
I look within and find joy.

INANNA, QUEEN OF EARTH

EL ÁRBOL DE LA VIDA / THE TREE OF LIFE

Good morning, Sun
Good morning, Earth
Good morning, Cool Mists
Good morning, Soft Breezes

I am Inanna:
I am daughter of the moon and queen of heaven;
Protector of the date palm oasis and full granaries;
My star in the heavens shines in the morning and in the evening.
I have returned from my sister Ereshkigal's cave.
I have come back into life.
I have returned to you.
In my hands once more are the powers granted me by the gods:

El puente de los colores

High, wide rainbows
Double and touching earth on both sides
Greet my homecoming.
Turning the corner into this new day
I stand facing east beneath shimmering colors.
With a bow and a salute
I greet the sun's rising

La entrada de la esperanza

I open wide the gate to my garden
Only to pause in prayer before entering.
There is plenty of time to greet its flowers,
Plenty of time to hold sun's bright stillness in my heart.

Beyond the gate
I see climbing scarlet roses and crushed silk hollyhocks of all colors.
As they spill their petals onto earth's rich black soil
I feel their welcoming joy. They mark a soft path for my feet.

In the inner courtyard
Flowering date palms, orange poppies, and night-blooming jasmine
Spill profligate scents into the air
To form clouds of encircling beauty.

Opening the gate to this garden
Reminds me of other gates, other paths.
I remember my journey's stark aloneness
Into barren, harsh horizons.

Crossing through my gate's threshold, I remember
This gate is not one of those gates. Here life embraces me.
Contentment holds me. Love welcomes me back.
This portal invites me to enter.

The garden beyond beckons me to other hidden paths
Filled with quiet peace.
Inside my courtyard, birds chatter.
My voice, full and bold, joins theirs.

I am earth's and sky's goddess and I sing.

El jardín mío del júbilo

As I watch, a small box turtle sticks its head out to taste
the dew:
Bees busily carry heavy golden pollen from a grove of
flowering citrus;
Crickets scuttle near the cedar trees;
Large orange and black butterflies mate in mid-air;
Tiny ants march in formation;
Hummingbirds sit in the tall huluppu tree:
In my heart, I hear the dolphins clicking to each other.
They welcome me back.

I am home.

A GUIDE TO SPANISH TITLES

Inanna's Journey: The Homeland

Cruzando la frontera: Crossing the border
El árbol sagrado del mundo: The sacred world tree
Los remolinos móviles de arena: Dust devils
Una canción pequeña para el viaje: A small song for the journey
Una frontera oscura: An obscure border
Hace muchos años: Many years ago
Empieza el viaje: The journey begins
El vendaval del norte: The strong north wind/gales
Raíz dulce: Sweet root
Una canción encantadora de la noche: An enchanted night song

Inanna's Journey: On Entering the Dark Wood:

Un árbol desapparecida: A disappeared tree
El umbral del bosque: The forest's threshold
El santo lugar: The shrine

The Dangerous Journey Below: The First Gate

La entrada primera: The first gate
Un dolor fuerte: A strong grief
Los días de los muertos: Days of the dead
Derramamiento de sangre: Spilling blood
Los terremotos grandes: Large earthquakes

The Dangerous Journey Below: The Second Gate

La entrada segunda: The second gate
La neblina: Mist
Bajo la lluvia: Under the rain
El viento cortante: The strong wind
Los sueños de la noche: Night dreams
Ruinas de las nieblas: Fog's ruins

La ventana abierta: The Open window
La estrella más brillante de la mañana: Venus, the morning star
Ritos de purificación: Purification rites
El portón abierto del jardín: The open garden gate

The Dangerous Journey Below: The Third Gate

La entrada tercera: The third gate
El portón grande: The large gate
Las aguas amargas: Bitter waters
La lluvia desnuda: Naked rain
El vendaval del sur: Strong south wind/gales
Raíces de los sueños oscuros: Root of hidden dreams
Lágrimas y chillidos: Tears and screams
Los estrechos del cañón: Canyon narrows
Una cascada grande: A large waterfall
Un puente de los recuerdos: A bridge of memories
La represión del río desenfrenado: Repression of frenzied waters
Las mareas más fuertes: Strong tides
El lugar del nacimiento del alma: The soul's birthplace
La mesa del sacrificio: The table of sacrifice
La catarata: Waterfall
No puede ser: It is not possible
Las tormentas llegan otra vez: Storms begin again
Portones filtrantes: Sluice gates
Mesa de la esperanza silenciosa:Table of silenced hope
Los obsequios: Gifts
El silencio espeso: Thick, fog-like silence

The Dangerous Journey Below: The Fourth Gate

La entrada cuarta: The fourth gate
La garrita cerrada: The closed guardhouse

The Dangerous Journey Below: The Fifth Gate

La entrada quinta: The fifth gate
El camino tortuoso: The crooked road

Una esquina de la noche: Night's corner
Los senderos despreciables: Despicable paths
La plata de la marisma: Swamp money

The Dangerous Journey Below: The Sixth Gate

La entrada sexta: The sixth gate
Memorias silenciadas: Silenced memories
Objetos y artefactos espirituales: Spiritual objects and artifacts
Documentos de identidad: Identity papers
Paredes de barro y portales de hierro: Mud walls and stone gates
Por vía de los sueños: Dream ways
Ojo de agua: Water's eye
Un sacrificio para los jueces: A sacrifice for the judges

The Dangerous Journey Below: The Seventh Gate

La entrada séptima: The seventh gate
El silencio gris y deprimente: Bleak silence
Bajo la sombra del sol: Under the sun's shadow
Las cataratas del terror: Terrifying cataracts
Cerro de la serpiente: Serpent hill
El jardín del sol caliente: Garden of the hot sun
La cueva sin salida: The cave with no exit
Los rápidos del dolor: Grief's whitewaters

Interlude

Una mujer moribunda: Dying woman
El tiempo del nacimiento del alma: The soul's birth time
Las ofrendas del mundo: The world's offerings
Reflexiones del mundo de los árboles de las sombras: Reflections from the world of the shadow trees
Mi hermana y mi enemiga: My sister and my enemy
Una mujer que nace: Birthing Woman
La matriz del tiempo consciente: The womb of consciousness
El momento en que se va la coronilla: The baby's crowning at birth
Dar a luz: Giving birth

The Homeland

Cruzando la frontera: Crossing the border
Una canción para el cielo: A song for the sky
Una canción para los océanos: A song for the world's oceans
Una canción para el bosque: A song for the forest
El árbol de la vida: The tree of life
Los puentes de los colores: Rainbow bridges
La entrada de la esperanza: Hope's doorway
El jardín mío del júbilo: My garden of joy

AFTERWORD

Times of change in our lives are often times of personal crisis. These times of crisis are filled with omens of danger for us. We sense this reality in our bones. They are, however, equally filled with opportunities for positive growth and transformation. However, the potential for personal transformation may remain hidden from our awareness unless we go in search for it.

In times of crisis we often lose touch with a secure and remembered sense of self that can serve to stabilize us as we journey through an intense time of change. So easily do we step out of balance and harmony. In these moments of inner imbalance and distress, we lose sight of ourselves. We lose awareness of the melody of joy that sustains us. We become so enmeshed in our struggles against the crisis which surrounds us that we can't recall or use our inner gyroscope. We find that familiar, previously well-worn pathways back to a personal sense of body and psyche integrity are blocked.

As current troubles pile upon ancient and unresolved troubles; as our losses accumulate: we often find ourselves increasingly isolated inside of our personal pain and suffering. In the middle of encountering new wounds, old wounds we thought were healed may break open once more. When this happens, our confusion, suffering and personal alienation increases. We forget who we are.

We begin to fear and doubt that we will ever again know spontaneous laughter, joy, and freedom. In the language of religious mysticism, we enter the *dark night of the soul*. In clinical language of contemporary healing systems, we enter a time of sickness, disease, pathology or illness.

In the great mythic traditions of our cultural heritage, we can find magical and lyrical stories about these times of human troubles. If we choose to look carefully enough, we can find in these ancient stories a certain revelatory moment that points the way towards a new path for us to follow.

In these mythic stories, the gods arbitrarily entangle a person in struggle and suffering. For the gods' own obscure and complex reasons, the fates and destiny have singled this person out for a heroic struggle with life itself. Persons so chosen, however, have no idea about why they were selected by the gods to make a journey into suffering and questioning. Feeling assaulted by life, these individuals lay wounded at the gate of death. Life has become intolerable and death terrifying. Trying to decide whether to die or to live, they sense that to begin a life worth living one more time, they must make a heroic journey into the depths of their spirit.

The ancient storytellers of these myths and legends warn their listeners that the outcomes of such a journey are never guaranteed. They warn all who set out on such a journey of recovering and remembering that the risks and dangers are high. They warn all who must face such a time of wandering, that it is possible to lose one's path in the forest.

Unlike the mythic hero who valiantly suffers all with patience and wins all, when we hear these legendary stories, we intuit that we might simply expand and extend the time of our suffering and that we may lose it all anyhow. We begin the journey, therefore, forewarned that we may sink into and become mired in our wounds.

Salvation, we know already, is denied to some and granted to others. Healing too is sometimes offered, sometimes denied. Yet it is never clear how the gods make this choice about whom to help and whom to abandon.

To onlookers who witness the journey, the random and hauntingly arbitrary descent of some into suffering appears nonsensical. In our personal survey of the horizons of suffering, not all who deserve to suffer do so. Living an apparently charmed life, they escape the suffering which encapsulates the life experience of others. As we look into the world of suffering we find that many who suffer much are innocent of the reasons for their fall from the gods' graces.

Brought into suffering by our life and its journeys, we eventually reach a place of multiple impasses. Any path which we can see in front of us appears to us as a wrong path. We are stuck. We cannot go back the way we came. We cannot see the path ahead of us. We resent the apparent "unfairness" of life. We call upon denial to manage our suffering. We call upon anger to mobilize our failing resources. To no avail!

Nevertheless, even in the middle of our suffering, life itself continues to call to us. We sense that we must move forward and that by our choices we will create our future. We encounter fears so ancient they have no reasonable names. In the silence of our suffering, we intuit an even deeper silence of healing. We open inner doors of the spirit – doors we previously had no knowing of – and we find new spaces in which to create and live our ongoing lives.

Encountering in our own personal experience (as if for the first time in human life) these ancient and archetypal stories, our naïve innocence is shattered. Our deepest intuitions tell us that once called by unknown voices to make such a journey, we cannot refuse. Thrown into suffering by the gods, the fates, or by life itself, we sense with a deep foreknowing that our life trajectory has been permanently changed.

In addition, we know with a deep wordless knowing that to have any hope of being re-born into wellness and wholeness, we must move into and through our pain. We must learn how to embrace it as our teacher. The journey into such a mythic dying to our previous self paradoxically becomes a journey into deep healing. Begun in suffering, this journey becomes nothing less than a passage into spiritual transformation of the individual.

In these times of suffering and confusion, something is there that must die in order that something new can be born. Something must be destroyed in order that something else can be created. Something must be shattered in order that something may become whole. This paradox is profound and inexplicable. We do not understand it. We simply come to know that this is true.

Looking into the deep places of anguish within, we know that insisting upon reclaiming our previous life (unexamined and unchanged) is the certain way into continuing disaster. Lost and not able to return the way that we have already traveled, we know we must search for a new path and a new journey.

The death of Eurydice and the subsequent journey of Orpheus into the realms of death; the abduction and rape of Persephone and the refusal of her mother Demeter to give up her maternal grief at the loss of her daughter; the descent of Jesus into hell to harrow it and rescue the dead; and the descent of Inanna into Ereshkigal's underground dust-filled cave: these and other stories teach us that journeying into the denied darkness can teach us much about life.

In my own encounter with the crisis of physical illness, I encountered *The Descent of the Goddess Inanna.* In my attempts to make sense of a body which I felt had betrayed me by not healing easily from a surgical wound, I found that Inanna's descent mirrored my own confusion about how to return to remembered wellness and wholeness. In my unspoken terror about future blindness I was lost in a forest and all around me were shadow trees. The path to healing appeared blocked no matter which direction I faced.

Needing to reconcile, in some manner, my own life's history with my hopes for the future, I needed to acknowledge what was dead or lost. I needed to encounter that which was still dying. To be born again, I responded with passionate identification to Inanna's own troubled and troubling journey. As a clinician and healer, I needed now to go in search of healing. I began the unwanted but necessary process of laying bare the suffering inside. A deeply private person about my inner world, I needed to open it to others' gazes for I needed their help.

In the story of Inanna's descent into the underworld of death and its shades, we find the story of Inanna's transformation. As she returns to life, earth's rich fecundity returns with her. Returning to life through the gates of death and loss, an ancient story of transformation and resurrection appears.

Now, fifteen years after my malignancy surgeries and their aftermath of an abdominal seroma, I have found my way back into life. Other serious illnesses have entered my life and I have needed medical care. Now continuing to live with an uncertain visual future, I have begun living in the present moment. Each day I am aware of the wonderful gift of seeing in this day, of living in this day. The practice of gratitude which I began inside the container of Emmet Miller's clinical practice has sustained me.

What I find each morning is such gratitude to the life force for sustaining me through my struggles to re-member and to re-order my life and journey. I find such abiding joy in the present moment of my life where earth's beauties surround me. I am, quite simply, delighted to be alive on planet earth.

What has surprised me the most is the spontaneously recurring comment from a wide variety of friends and colleagues: *these days you seem so much more at peace with yourself.* When I pause with them, I understand that they rightly perceive some vast changes in my inner world. I am growing in patience. I am growing in gratitude. I am growing in acceptance of that which is (as opposed to being greedy for what is not).

There has been trauma in my life. I am much less victimized by its history in my life than I was in 1995 – when my surgically altered body spoke a simple message to me: *Pay Attention! This time in your life is very important. Don't miss the opportunity to learn, grow, and change.*

By creating the manuscript and masks of *Inanna's Way*, I began to tell the story of my wounds and of my strong desire to regain a full and joyous life. My particular story as a particular woman blends into Inanna's archetypal story of violence, illness, loss, suffering and dys-ease. In beginning to share the poetry and masks outside of my immediate friendship group, I found that these themes became visible to others as they too dealt with various forms of personal suffering.

During the past several years (while the *Inanna's Way* poetry and mask photographs rested on my office shelves) I kept asking myself and I kept asking colleagues and friends, *Is this simply a personal story for close friends and family to understand?* In an elongated process of questioning my own motives for releasing the story into a different world than the private one, I decided that if Inanna's story or my own story could be useful to other women and men who have lost their own sense of a trusted and beloved body, then it was important to leave behind my intense personal sense of privacy in order that those who needed her story could hear the story of the goddess Inanna for themselves.

April 10, 2016

APPENDIX: REFERENCE WORKS

COMPANY FOR THE ROAD

As we journey in and through the troubled times of our lives, we search for healing. In that search, we long for those who can and will accompany us. We search for people to journey with us and to understand us as we struggle to find or to create our own path in the worlds of illness, pain, confusion, loss and grief. In addition to friends and healers, some of us turn also to the worlds of books, music and the visual arts. In our sifting through these diverse universes of image, metaphor and symbol, we create a unique and particular matrix of meaning. It is inside this matrix that we eventually come to understand the meaning of illness and the meaning of healing to our own bodySelf. In its simplest and purest essence, it is this matrix that undergirds and structures the healing process as we experience it.

Others in search of meaning, understanding and healing would most certainly find their personal and unique set of resources. Yet, as I have talked about my own descent into illness and my continuing return to wholeness, I have discovered that others want to know what has happened to me. They ask me what I have learned about the processes of re-balancing and re-grounding my life.

The list below documents some of the resources I consulted in my own search of a path into healing. I share them with you in the hope that in your own troubled times, you might be reminded to search out your own unique mix of authors, musicians, artists, and healers to accompany you as you journey into and through your troubles.

INANNA AND HER WORLD

Baring, A. and Cashford, J. (1991). *The Myth of the Goddess: Evolution of an Image.* London, UK: Arkana/Penguin.

Bonneton, Y. with W. Doniger. (1991). *Mythologies.* Chicago, IL: University of Chicago.

Cahill, S. M. (1996). Hymn in Praise of the Goddess Ishtar of Babylonia (pp. 3-5) in S. M. Cahill, Susan M. (Ed.). *Wise Women: Over 5000 Years of Spiritual Writing by Women.* New York, NY: W.W. Norton.

Farber, W. (1985). Witchcraft, Magic and Divination in Ancient Mesopotamia (pp. 1895-1909) in J. M. Sassen (Ed.) *Civilizations of the Ancient Near East.* New York, NY: Charles Scribner's Sons.

Gilbert, A. S. (1985). The Flora and Fauna of the Ancient Near East (pp. 153-174) in J. M. Sassen (Ed.). *Civilization of the Ancient Near East.* New York, NY: Charles Scribner's Sons.

Glassner, J.-J. (1985). The Use of Knowledge in Ancient Mesopotamia (pp. 1815-1823) in J. M. Stassen (Ed.). *Civilization of The Near East.* New York, NY: Charles Scribner's Sons.

Hastings, J. (Ed.). (1951). *Encyclopedia of Religion and Ethics.* New York, NY: Scribners.

James, E. O. (1978). *The Ancient Gods.* London, UK: Weidenfeld and Nicholson, 1978.

Kramer, S. N. (1967). *Cradle of a Civilization.* New York, NY: Time-Life Books; (1961). *History Begins at Sumer.* London, UK: Thames and Hudson; (1944). *Sumerian Mythology.* Philadelphia, PA:

American Philosophical Society memoirs, volume 27, pp. 89-93; (1989) *Myth of Enki: The Crafty God.* New York, NY: Oxford.

Kramer, S. N. (Ed). (1961). *Mythologies of the Ancient World.* Garden City, NJ: Doubleday, pp. 93-137.

Lambert, W. G. (1995). Myth and Myth Making in Sumer and Akkad (pp. 1825-1835) in J. M. Sassen (Ed.) *Civilizations of the Ancient Near East.* New York, NY: Charles Scribner's Sons.

Leach, M. (1992). *Guide to the Gods.* Santa Barbara, CA: ABC-CLIO.

Meador, B. De Shong (2000). *Inanna, Lady of Largest Heart: Poems of the Sumerian High Priestess Enheduanna.* Austin, TX: University of Texas Press.

Pritchard, J. B. (Ed.). (1961. *Ancient Near Eastern Texts Relating to the Old Testament, 3rd edition with Supplement.* Princeton, NJ: Princeton University Press.

Renfrew, J. M. (1995). Vegetables in the Ancient Near Eastern Diet (pp. 191-202) in J. M. Sassen (Ed.). *Civilizations of the Ancient Near East.* New York, NY: Charles Scribner's Sons.

Sanders, N.K. (1960). *The Epic of Gilgamesh.* Middlesex, UK: Penguin Books.

Scurlock, J. (1995). Death and the Afterlife in Mesopotamian Thought (pp. 1883-1893). In J. M. Sassen, Ed. *Civilizations of the Ancient Near East.* New York, NY: Charles Scribner's Sons.

Starhawk (1987). *Truth or Dare: Encounters with Power, Authority, and Mystery.* San Francisco, CA: Harper and Row.

Stern, E., et. al. (1993). *The New Encyclopedia of Archeological Explorations in the Holy Land.* New York, NY: Simon and Schuster.

Waldherr, K. (1995). *The Book of the Goddesses.* Hillsboro, OR: Beyond Words.

Wolkstein, D. and Kramer, S. N. (1983). *Inanna: Queen of Heaven and Earth: Her Stories and Hymns.* New York, NY: Harper and Row.

WOMEN HEALERS ENCOUNTER INANNA

Bolen, J. S. (1994). *Crossing to Avalon: A Woman's Midlife Pilgrimage.* San Francisco, CA: Harper and Row; (1996). *Close to the Bone: Life-Threatening Illness and the Search for Meaning.* New York, NY: Scribners.

Reis, P. (1991). *Through the Goddess: A Woman's Way of Healing.* New York, NY: Continuum.

Perera, S. (1981). *Descent to the Goddess: A Way of Initiation For Women.* Toronto, Canada: Inner City Books.

Weiner, S. with H. Smith. (Fall 1994/Winter 1995). A Tale of Two Sisters (pp. 8-10) in *Ways of the Healer.* San Francisco, CA: Program of Medicine and Philosophy, California Pacific Medical Center.

VISUAL REPRESENTATIONS OF INANNA

Austin, H. I. (1990). *The Heart of the Goddess: Art, Myth, and Meditations of the World's Sacred Feminine.* Berkeley, CA: Wingbow.

Blair, N. (1995). *Goddesses for Every Season.* Rockport, MA: Elements Press.

Boulet, S. S., with M. Babcock (1997). *The Goddess Paintings.* San Francisco, CA: Pomegranate Books.

Boulet, S. S. (1997). *Goddesses: The Paintings of Susan Seddon Boulet.* Rohnart Park, CA: Pomegranate Books.

GENERAL WORKS ABOUT MYTHOLOGY AND SYMBOL

Apostolos-Cappadona, D. (1966). *Encyclopedia of Women in Religious Art.* New York, NY: Continuum.

Bachofen, J. J. with an introduction by Joseph Campbell (1993). *Myth, Religion, and Mother Right: Selected Writings of J.J. Bachofen.* Princeton, NJ: Princeton University Press Bollingen Series.

Black, J. and Green, A. (1992). *Gods, Demons, and Symbols of Ancient Mesopotamia: An Illustrated Dictionary.* Austin, TX: University of Texas at Austin Press.

Campbell, J. (1968). *The Hero with a Thousand Faces.* Princeton, NJ: Princeton University Press.

Campbell, J. (1976). *The Masks of God: Occidental Mythology.* New York, NY: Penguin Books.

Campbell, J. (1972). *Myths to Live By.* New York, NY: Bantam.

Downing, C. (1984). *The Goddess: Mythological Images of The Feminine.* New York, NY: Crossroad.

Eliade, M. (Ed.). (1987). *The Encyclopedia of Religion.* New York, NY: Macmillan.

Estes, C. P. (1997). *Warming the Stone Child: Myths and Stories about Abandonment and the Unmothered Child.* Boulder, CO: Sounds True Audio.

Forty, J. (1999). *Mythology: A Visual Encyclopedia.* London, UK: PRC.

Frazier, J. G. (1963). *The Golden Bough.* New York, NY: Macmillan.

Gimbutas, M. (1992). *The Goddesses and Gods of Old Europe, 6500-3500 B.C.:Myths and Cult Images.* Berkeley, CA: University of California Press.

Gimbutas, M. (1989). *The Language of the Goddess.* San Francisco, CA: Harper and Row Publishers.

Gimbutas, M. with M. R. Dexter (Ed.). (2001). *The Living Goddesses* Berkeley, CA: University of California Press.

Gimbutas, M. with J. Campbell (2001. *The Language of the Goddess.* London, UK: Thames and Hudson.

Glueck, N. (1966). *Deities and Dolphins: The Story of the Nabataeans.* London, UK: Cassell.

Goodrich, N. L. (1960). *The Ancient Myths.* New York, NY: The New American Library of World Literature.

Graves, R. (1968). Introduction in F. Gulrand (Ed.). *The New Larousse Encyclopedia of Mythology.* Paris, France: The Librarie Larousse.

Graves, R. and Patai, R. (1964). *Hebrew Myths: The Book of Genesis.* Garden City, NY: Doubleday and Company.

Graves, R. (1966). *The White Goddess: A Historical Grammar of Poetic Myth.* New York, NY: Farrar, Straus, Giroux.

Hall, J. (1974). *Dictionary of Subjects and Symbols in Art.* San Francisco, CA: Harper and Row.

Hall, N. (1980). *The Moon and the Virgin: Reflections on the Archetypal Feminine.* New York, NY: Harper and Colophon.

Harding, M. E. (1973). *Women's Mysteries.* New York, NY: Bantam.

Jacobson, T. (1976). *The Treasures of Darkness: A History of Mesopotamian Religion.* New Haven, CT: Yale University Press.

Jordon, M. (1993). *Encyclopedia of Gods.* New York, NY: Facts on File.

Judith, A. (1996). *Wheels of Life: A User's Guide to the Chakra System.* St. Paul, MN: Llewellyn Publications.

Jung, C. G. (1997). *Man and his Symbols.* Laure Leaf.

Liungman, C. G. (1991). *Dictionary of Symbols.* Santa Barbara, CA: ABC-CLIO.

Neuman, E. (1972). *The Great Mother: An Analysis of the Archetype.* Princeton, NJ: Princeton University Press.

Ochshorn, J. (1981). *The Female Experience and the Nature of the Divine.* Bloomington, IN: University of Indiana Press.

Patai, R. (1976). *The Hebrew Goddess.* New York, NY: Avon.

Stone, M. (1976). *When God was a Woman.* New York, NY: Harcourt, Brace Jovanovich.

Walker, B. G. (1988). *The Woman's Dictionary of Symbols and Sacred Objects.* San Francisco, CA: Harper and Row.

Walker, B. G. (1983). *The Woman's Encyclopedia of Myths and Secrets.* San Francisco, CA: Harper and Row.

SPIRITUAL GUIDES AND MEDICAL HEALERS

Achterberg, J. (1990). *Woman as Healer.* Boston: Shambhala.

Achterberg, J. and Dossey, B., and Kolkmeier, L. (1994). *Rituals of Healing: Using Imagery for Health and Wellness.* New York, NY: Bantam Books.

Benson, H. with M. Stark. (1997). *Timeless Healing: The Power and Biology of Belief.* New York, NY: Firestone.

Bolen, J. S. (1982). *The Tao of Psychology: Synchronicity and the Self.* San Francisco, CA: Harper.

Capacchione, L. (1990). *The Picture of Health: Healing Your Life with Art.* Santa Monica, CA: Hay House; (1989). *The Power of Your Other Hand.* North Hollywood, CA: Newcastle Publishing Company; (1989). *Drawing on Your Inner Power to Heal Yourself.* North Hollywood, CA: Newcastle Publishing Company.

Chodron, P. (1995). *Awakening Compassion: Meditation Practices for Difficult Times.* Boulder, CO: Sounds True Audio; (1994). *Start Where You Are: A Guide to Compassionate Living.* Boston, MA: Shambhala; (1997). *When Things Fall Apart: Heart Advice for Difficult Times.* Boston, MA: Shambhala.

Elliott, T. S. (1943). *Four Quartets* (1943). New York, NY: Harcourt, Brace Jovanovich.

Estes, C. P. *Warming the Stone Child: Myths and Stories about Abandonment and the Unmothered Child.* Boulder, CO: Sounds True.

Kabat-Zinn, J. (1990). *Full Catastrophe Living: Using the Wisdom of Your Body and Mind to Face Stress, Pain and Illness.* New York, NY: Delta.

LeShan, L. (1990). *Cancer as a Turning Point: A Handbook For People with Cancer, their Families, and Health Professionals.* New York, NY: Plume.

Levine, S. (1997). *A Year to Live: How to Live This Year as if It Were Your Last.* New York, NY: Bell Tower; (1982). *Who Dies: An Investigation of Conscious Living and Dying.* New York, NY: Anchor Books.

May, R. (1976). *Courage to Create.* New York, NY: W. W. Norton.

Miller, A. (1991). *Breaking Down the Wall of Silence: The Liberating Experience of Facing Painful Truth.* New York, NY: Penguin/Dutton; (1980a). *The Drama of the Gifted Child.* New York, NY: Basic Books; (1983). *For Your Own Good: Hidden Cruelty in Child-rearing and the Roots of Violence.* New York, NY: Farrar, Straus, and Giroux; (1980b). *The Untouched Key: Tracing Childhood Trauma in Creativity and Destructiveness,* (H. and H. Hnnum, Trans.). New York, NY: Doubleday.

Miller, E. E. (1995). *Deep Healing: The Healing Journey Within.* Boulder, CO: Sounds True Audio; (1996). *Deep Healing.* Carlsbad, CA: Hay House; *Healing Journey.* Menlo Park, CA: Source Cassette Learning System; *Rainbow Butterfly.* Menlo Park, CA: Source Cassette Learning System.

Miller, E. E. with S. Halpren. (1998). *Letting Go of Stress.* Menlo Park, CA: Source Cassette Learning System.

Miller, E. E. with D. Leuth (1986). *Self Imagery: Creating Your Own Good Health.* Berkeley, CA: Celestial Arts.

Muller, W. (1993). *Legacy of the Heart: The Spiritual Advantages of a Painful Childhood.* New York, NY: Simon and Schuster.

Oliver, M. (1992). *New and Selected Poems.* Boston, MA: Beacon Press.

Nepo, M. (2000). *The Book of Awakening: Having the Life You Want by Being Present to the Life You Have.* Berkeley, CA: Conari; (1986). *Inside the Miracle: Enduring Illness, Approaching Wholeness.* Parabola Audio Library and the Society for the Study of Myth and Tradition.

Nhat Hanh, T. (1981). *Being Peace.* Berkeley, CA: Parallax Press; (1993). *Call Me By My True Names: The Collected Poems of Thich Nhat Hanh.* Berkeley, CA: Parallax Press; (1995). *Living Buddha, Living Christ.* New York, NY: Riverhead Books.

Remen, R. N. (1996). Front-Row Seat (pp. 15-17) in *Kitchen Table Wisdom: Stories that Heal.* New York, NY: Riverhead; (2000). *My Grandfather's Blessings: Stories of Strength, Refuge and Belonging.* New York, NY: Riverhead; (1994). *Wounded Healers: A Book of Poems by People who have had Cancer and Those Who Love and Care for Them.* Mill Valley, CA.

Rossman, M. L. (1987). *Healing Yourself.* New York, NY: Pocket Books of Simon and Schuster.

MUSIC TO CALM AND INFORM THE SPIRIT

In the process of dealing with my fears, I found that sometimes music was the only way I could make my way into my quiet inner space where healing imagery could emerge. The following works were very much a part of the journey to healing and they accompanied the creation of poetry and masks as an integral aspect of regaining inner balance. In the presence of almost continuous music, I found an inner sense that I would eventually be restored to mySelf. During this sabbatical year when I was preoccupied with issues of healing, I eventually learned to surround myself with clouds of soft music. At times I sang. At others, I danced. I began to learn how to play with my moods; my despair, my fears, my grief, my anger and eventually my joy and exhilaration. Making music and listening to music became a daily part of the life's journey back to a re-balanced awareness of hope, and contentment.

Bizet, Georges "Au fond du temple saint" from *Les Pecheurs de Perles* on Hadley and Hampson: The Orchestra of Welsh National Opera with Carlo Rizzi conducting/9031-73283-2 (Germany: Teldec, A Time-Warner Compaany, 1993).

Brahms, Johannes, "Denn alles Fleisch, es wie Gras" and Ihr habt nun Taurigkeit" from *Ein deutsches Requiem* with Andre Previn conducting the Royal Philharmonic/ 9031-75862-2 (Germans: Teldec Classics, 1987).

Choir of the New College Oxford with Edward Higginbottom Conducting, *Agnus Dei*/0630-14634-2 (Paris, France, 1996).

Choir of the Vienna Hofburgkapelle with Josef Schabasser Conducting, *Mystical Chants*/SCD 5118 (Englewood Cliffs, NJ: Special Music Company, 1994).

Coxon, Robert, *The Silent Path*/RHc-CCD-5501 (Westmount, Quebec, Canada, SOCAN, 1995).

Coyote Oldham, *Tear of the Moon* (Norman, OK: Coyote Oldham Music, 1987).

Darling, David, *Cello*/314-511-982-2 (Munich, Germany: ECM Records, 1992).

Domingo, Placido, "An American Hymn: Main Theme" from *East of Eden* on *Perhaps Love*/MK37243 (NY: CBS Records Masterworks, 1991).

Enya, *The Memory of Trees*/946106-2 (UK: Warner Music, 1995).

Gardner, Kay, *A Rainbow Path* (Durham, NC: Ladyslipper, Inc., 1984).

Gilbert, Ronnie, "Music in My Mother's House," on Holly Near and Ronnie Gilbert, *This Train Still Runs*/AAHO696 (Berkeley, CA: Abbe Alice Music, 1996).

Goodal, Medwyn, *The Way of the Dolphin*/NWCD 220 (Suffolk, UK: New World Music, 1992).

Goodal, Medwyn, *Medicine Woman*/NWCD229 (Suffolk, UK: New World Music, 1992).

Goodal, Medwyn, *Moon Goddess*/NWCCD 409 (Suffolk, UK: New World Music, 1996).

Halpern, Steven, *Crystal Suite*/SRXD7842 (San Anselmo, CA: Steve Halpern's Inner Peace Music, 1986).

Handel, George Frederic, "Dank sie Dir" on *Classical Barbra*/MK33452 (Tokyo, Japan: CBS Masterworks, Inc., 1976).

Jones, Michael, *Seascapes*/CD-1004 (Milwaukee, WI: Narada, 1984).

Jones, Michael, *Sunscape*/CD-1009 (Milwaukee, WI: Narada, 1985).

Jones, Michael, *Touch*/ND61057 (Milwaukee, WI: Narada, 1996).

Jones, Michael and David Darling, *Amber*/ND61014 (Milwaukee, WI: Narada, 1987).

Lanz, David, *Beloved*/ND64009 (Milwaukee, WI: Narada, 1995).

Lanz, David and Paul Speer, *Desert Vision*/ND63003 (Milwaukee, WI: Narada, 1987).

McDade, Carolline and Friends, *Sorrow and Healing* (Carlisle, MA: Blue Jay Recording, 1993).

McKennitt, Lorena, *The Mask and the Mirror*/9-45420-2 (Stratford, Ontario, Canada: Quinton Road, Ltd., 1994).

Mozart, Wolfgang Amadeus, "Clarinet Concerto in A-KV 622" on Mozart/422-390-2 with Sir Neville Mariner and the Academy of St. Martin in the Fields (NY: Phillips, 1989).

Nakai, Carlos, *Canyon Trilogy* (Phoenix, AZ: Canyon Record Productions, Inc., 1989).

Native Flute Ensemble, *Gathering of Shaman*/TT1190D (San Antonio, X: Talking Taco Records, 1993).

Norman, Jessye, *Amazing Grace*/432-546-2 (NY: Phillips, 1991).

Rainer, John, Jr., *Songs of the Indian Flute* (Orem, UT: Red Willow Songs, 1986).

Roos, Anne and Bionski, David, *Through the Mist/RB 501 CD* (Garden Valley, CA: Timeless Productions, 1993).

Taize Community, *Allelujah*/CD194 (Chicago, IL: GIA Distributors, 1988).

Taize Community, *Jubilate*/GIACD284 (Chicago, IL: GIA Distributors, 1991).

Taize Community, *Veni Sancte Spiritus*/CD325 (Chicago, IL: GIA Distributors, 1994).

Taylor, James, "Only One" on *James Taylor Live*/7464-47056-2 (NY: Columbia, 1993).

Winston, George, *Forest*/01934-11157-2 (Stanford, CA: Windham Hill Records, 1994).

ABOUT THE AUTHOR

Dr. Ruth Elizabeth Krall, Emerita Professor of Religion, Psychology and Nursing, and Program Director of Peace, Justice, and Conflict Studies at Goshen College, Indiana. Born and raised in Pennsylvania, she earned a bachelor of nursing from Goshen College, IN, a masters from the University of Cincinnati, OH, and a PhD from the Southern California School of Theology at Claremont. She also worked as a psychiatric community health, nurse and currently lives in Arizona as a retired pastoral theologian specialized in sexual violence studies. A Mennonite with Methodist membership, her ecumenical approach provides pathways of successful nonviolent advocacy in situations of affinity, sexual violations and armed violence. Throughout her professional career she has had direct and personal contact with hundreds of survivors of sexual abuse, domestic abuse, and war. The outline of her earlier contributions as a feminist can be read in *Feminists Who Changed America: 1963 to 1975*, published in 2006 by Barbara J. Love.

Archival holdings can be found at the Mennonite Historical Library at Goshen College, Mennonite Church USA Archives (Elkhart, IN), and the Pacific School of Religion at UC Berkeley. Ruth Krall maintains a website where many of her writings can be downloaded free of charge. www.enduringspace.com She first presented the Inanna poems at a meeting of the Midwest AAR in Chicago. Someone in attendance invited her to present them at a psychology conference in Vancouver, BC.

www.ingramcontent.com/pod-product-compliance
Lightning Source LLC
Chambersburg PA
CBHW031350230926
51848CB00002B/458